Praise for *The Girl Who Dances With Delight*

To read this book is to follow a pathway of glittering crumbs to the forgotten city of the Self. It leads the way to radical self love & self awareness and sparkling soul with the voice of a trusted friend and a soundtrack that sings life awake! We follow her because delight awaits us around every curve. Every daily dance brings us closer to our own delighted spirits! I look forward to the companionship of this book, flipping it open for inspiration for years to come!
~ **Julia Alter** Creative Force at Seize the Dazzle Studio
Artist, Poet, & Author of *Walking the Hot Coal of the Heart*

So much more than a guide to a daily ritual, this book invites us to open our eyes and hearts to new ways of seeing and being, using the acronym D.A.N.C.E, and associated activities, as a guide. Julia's vulnerability and honesty encourage us to be and express ourselves freely and without reservation. I've incorporated the DANCE ritual into my life and, in just a short time, have almost magically received myriad benefits for my body, mind and soul. I'm grateful for Julia's courage and willingness to share a beautiful process with the world.
~ **Kerri Aab** Fitness Instructor, Wellness Coach, Mental Health Advocate and Complex PTSD Thriver

This book is inspiring, well-written, engaging, fun, nourishing and truly a pleasure to read! It is the ultimate guidebook for cultivating self-love, self-nourishment and self-discovery. It will enhance your sense of wonder, appreciation, and joy in each moment regardless of the circumstances you may currently be facing in life. Julia's DANCE steps will inspire you, guide you, and help you feel deeply connected to your own radiant soul.
~ **Corinne Zupko, Ed. S.** Author of *From Anxiety to Love*
Counselor, Coach, Professor, and Mindfulness Instructor

Julia's love and exuberance for life shines brightly in each sweet daily chapter. She shares deeply and personally about her journey, her joys, her sorrows, her highs and her lows. You feel you are sharing an intimate conversation with a dear friend. I love how she weaves her story with a multitude of songs from every genre. After reading, I began to dance daily to greet the day. I loved her book so much that I bought two of them, one for me and another for a dear soul sister who I know will love to D.A.N.C.E. with Delight.

~ **Janette Stuart**
Author of the *On A Path Of Joy* Series of seven Devotional Books

This gorgeous gem of beauty, light and wisdom from an equally gorgeous author-artist-soul is something you should not miss. From the opening poem, through the many magical, delicious daily rituals, to the D.A.N.C.E. steps and closing words, we're invited to lighten up, liven up and vibrate with joy! This book is truly a gift. Through its pages I quickly and unapologetically recognize myself as a kindred sacred fool on this wild ride!

~ **Laura Di Franco, MPT** Holistic Physical Therapist, Poet, and Author of 6 books, including *Brave Healing, A Guide for Your Journey*

What a refreshing approach to living life on our terms! Julia gives us precious tools with her lovely D.A.N.C.E. prompts to hear the music over the loudness of fears (Face Everything And Recover). Life gets messy, hard, sad, scary, and at times, downright painful. Julia helps us shift out of the accepted drudgery to experience more joy in our lives. I have a tendency to be a little over serious. So, it is a true blessing to have the guidance offered within to help us stay more in the light, the true intelligence of the heart.

~ **Jeanette MacDonald** Artist & Author of *Lady And The Fox*

With delightful curiosity, Julia invites readers to explore freedom of movement to support change and transformation in life. I love the way she connects this process with thoughtful inquiries, stories, song lyrics, life lessons, and affirmations. Each unique chapter of the guided D.A.N.C.E. practice makes choosing joy flow more naturally. Let this be a companion for your beautiful daily journey on Earth guided by the moon and stars.

~ **April Miller McMurtry** Founder of The Moon Is My Calendar
and Creator of the *New Moon Calendar Journal*

The Girl Who

DANCES

With DeLight

Also by Julia Ostara:

Heart of Life Inspiration Card Deck

Soul Songs Inspiration Card Deck

Thrivival Online Creative Courses

Painting Prayers Online Course

Original Art, Art Prints, & Gifts

www.ThriveTrue.com

The Girl Who

DANCES

With DeLight

Liven Up
Lighten Up
Let Your Heart Sing

Daily Rhythm, Ritual, & Enrichment

Julia Ostara

www.ThriveTrue.com

ISBN: 978-1-7323974-2-2
1st Edition, June 2018

Library of Congress Control Number: 2018906686

Cover Art:
Luna's Tears (original painting digitally altered for book cover)
By Julia Ostara © 2018
May the tides replenish the tears & refill the well within.

DEDICATION

To Mother Mystery, the Wonder, Beauty, and Joy in Life

To my Angel Momma, Paulette, who taught me to dance in
sunshine, dance in the rain, and on into the mystic.
Yes, I still dance with her!

To my Dad, Bill, who asked my Mom to dance
and kept dancing with her until her last breath.

To Jane, who joins my Dad back out on the dance floor now.

To Nathan, who fills our home & my heart with music.

For my boys, Evan & Drew, who make my soul sing!

For all of us learning the steps as we go.

For YOU!

May we each find ways to Dance in Harmony with Delight.

CONTENTS

Let there be Dancing

~ Julia Ostara

Would you like to come inside
From the chills of a bitter world?

Bring all the tears you've shed
To be turned into wine.

A toast to your Courage!
Come on inside.

Warm your strong, soft, Sacred Spirit
By the Eternal Fire of Mother Love.

Listen to the Divine Song
As the crickets and the Angels serenade us.
Shall we sing along?

Let us Open our Hearts
To appreciate this Holy Ground
As it nourishes and holds us.

Drink from the shimmering dew.
Taste the sweet golden honey.

Breathe in the apple blossoms.
Have you savored the delicious fruit?

Let us feel the kiss of the ancient mist
Gently caress our temple bodies

Let us play in the dappled sunlight
At the edge of time.

Let us wander this rich Earth
With bare feet to
Explore Nature's Cathedral.

Feel the life flowing
Full and Free.

Let us open our wings
To glide with the
Wind of Change

While sailing in an
Ocean of Grace.

Let us Grow like Wildflowers
Each new dawn

As this Magic Moment invites us
To join the Celebration
And Dance with Delight.

Oh, let us Open our arms to Embrace
Gifts of beauty, wonder, and joy

Let Heaven Shine through us.

Let us Trust the Stardust
That sparkles in our eyes.

Let us see ourselves
In the moonlight and

Behold the Divine Within us.

PREFACE

Life can be such a wild rollercoaster ride of ups and downs! It can be so beautiful and yet so bittersweet. Even as a relatively young child and even though I was blessed with loving parents, I knew what it was like to feel betrayed, afraid, and alone. Even though I remember running wild through the woods and loving the summer sparkles from fireflies in the fields, I don't recall feeling as carefree as the memories seem to suggest for long. As my innocence was taken or lost, life felt heavier and more serious.

I drew the 'Sacred Fool' oracle card from a deck by Alana Fairchild as I was writing this book. At first, I was a bit resistant to that card. After considering it more and reading through the information in the accompanying guide book, I loved it! It was about having high hopes and expecting great things regardless of what anyone might say to discourage us or in spite of the odds. It makes me think of lightening up, as in not taking life or myself too seriously.

I realize that's not always easy to do. When the rollercoaster goes flying downwards or gets off track, life can be overwhelming! If we have health concerns or high stress, we might feel that life is very serious indeed. The year before I wrote this book, I had some scary health issues. I had a lot of abnormal bleeding. I was exhausted and nervous. What if I had ovarian cancer like my mom did? I started going to doctors and having tests. I was monitored and tested for several months as the symptoms continued.

During that time, I also started doing the morning ritual shared in this book on a more regular basis. I had been doing many of the activities off and on for a long time. After creating an acronym and becoming more intentional with the morning steps, I started doing it daily. I also had friends I've never even met in person sending me distance Reiki energy healing and lots of prayers and well wishes. Before the doctors were able to figure out what was causing the problems, the scary symptoms disappeared! The ultrasounds and other follow-up tests no longer showed abnormalities either.

I don't know if the magical morning D.A.N.C.E. had anything to do with the healing, but it definitely made me feel better even when I was too tired to do much movement. It also helped heal my spirit.

I wonder how many dis-eases and illnesses are caused by stress, pressure, anxiety, doubt, and depression. The country I live in is one of the most heavily drugged in the world. I accepted cultural ideas that life was about 'survival of the fittest' and 'life is hard' for much of my life. Yet, I watch the songbirds and the deer and the dragonflies and I wonder. Is it really the case? Must it be that way?

So, I'm trying an experiment. I'm willing to be a 'Sacred Fool.' I'm choosing to lean in to the joy and dance with delight amidst the drama, strife, surviving, striving, and suffering. I'm still able to find beauty and sweetness within and around me.

I wonder how kids might feel if we started schools with a morning ritual similar to the D.A.N.C.E. that I do. I don't remember doing anything like this way back when I was in school. I don't recall learning much about affirmations, self respect, reverence for life, or celebrating beauty and gratitude aside from giving the customary thanks for food. I think I would have benefitted from something like this, especially as a teen. It would have been pretty cool to start the day this way back when I worked in the corporate world also.

I welcome people of all backgrounds to this dance party!

After a winding road and a few dark nights, I've learned to love and respect myself and life. I love having the ability to see, share, create, and celebrate deep beauty, kindness, variety, wonder, and joy in this wild world. I think this is now part of my essence and life's work. Thankfully, I have learned to Dance with Delight. It feels so much better than dwelling too much on the drudgery in the world. It also motivates me to be more encouraging and generous. I've learned to liven up and lighten up! I've decided to let my heart sing. I hope to be a girl who dances with delight for the rest of my days.

To me, Delight is the strong Sacred Spark within each of us.

This book was written with Delight by the warmth of winter fires, cuddled up in a cozy loveseat, with bare feet sitting on the porch by a goldfish pond, with spring sun setting through the trees, in the dark as dreamy scribbles by the bedside, outdoors as frost melted, peach trees blossomed, ferns unfurled, wrens hatched, roses filled the air with a heavenly scent and strawberries ripened, and while dancing! I kept a notebook nearby while dancing so those notes also went into the book. It came alive and grew in rhythm with the seasons. The wonderful, beautiful, natural, lively energy and vibes are secret ingredients. I let Delight lead this song and Dance.

I share the stories and spiritual practices because I've been inspired by others that have done the same, and I trust the potential. I share as if having an intimate conversation by the fire rather than writing a paper for an English class in school, which were not my highest grades! My husband said it felt like the book should be written in poems. So, I was inspired to write the opening and closing poems to wrap it up in a poetic hug. I hope it will bring a soft smile to your spirit and bless your sweet heart, as they say here in the South.

In Harmony,

Jules

Julia Ostara
ThriveTrue.com

INTRODUCTION

It's a magical day for a moon dance... every day of our lives!

This sweet little book is about falling in love with ourselves and with life. In this book, I share ways that I've added rhythm, ritual, and enrichment to lighten my days while Dancing with Life and Letting my Heart Sing. I share a daily ritual that has had a beautiful impact on my life. I've come to think of ritual as something that enriches our lives, our environment, or our community due to the attention and action we give it. I've even made up my own word, as I often do, to combine enrich and ritual: enritchual. I'm probably not the first to do so, but I haven't found it in a dictionary yet.

I've noticed ritual was missing in my life for a long time. The main rituals and ceremonies I knew of were for birthdays, graduations, weddings, and funerals. I didn't have a way of celebrating the magic and beauty and reverence for everyday stuff. I've noticed it makes a difference in my daily life to have a simple way to appreciate it more. It doesn't need to be anything fancy. It definitely doesn't need to be long, dull, rote, traditional, or boring to qualify. Now, I tend to greet life as both a temple and a playground.

I invite you to dance with me, with your own strong, soft Sacred Spirit, with Life and Delight. The word D.A.N.C.E. is an acronym reminder for the basic steps of a ritual I do most mornings, yet anytime is a good time! I admit that I'm not naturally a bright eyed morning person. It's rejuvenating to add more fluid movement.

This book is a way for me to 'take the lead' as a dance partner for a while. You could think of it like a dance camp. I share my intuitive daily ritual with many variations to guide you in the process. You'll find plenty of possibilities through examples, ideas, and prompts each day for about a month. You can go at your own pace and trust your own rhythm. You can improvise, make it your own and keep on 'dancing' long after you finish the book!

Dancing is often a rather intimate experience. I share many stories from my own life throughout this monthly moon dance together. I think of the many generations before us who shared stories and dancing around the fire. May we fan the flames of delight!

I've become a sort of medicine collector and explorer. I use the word medicine similar to how some Native Americans do and like laughter is good medicine! It's soul food and spirit medicine. It can enrich and enlighten our lives. I share personal stories, experiences, and explorations of many ideas from a vast collection of wisdom, traditions, and sources along with my own intuition. I share with a collective voice. I'm grateful for all of the messengers and mentors.

I love how muses often sing to me through music! I sing and dance along with many great songs throughout this book. My mom said I started singing along with music before I started talking. Maybe that explains why I often think in songs! Though the songs I share may be too cultural or generational, I'm still including them. Stories and songs have been a way of communicating wisdom and wonder and connecting for so long through bards and elders and around fires. This is my modern way of doing that by mixing in references to books, television shows, movies, and songs that we may have in common. I invite you to sing along! Some of my favorite songs aren't mentioned, and I'm surprised at some that are. I let whatever flowed forth from the radio station in my head be shared as the various topics prompted different songs to play. There are music playlists and many other resources at the end of the book if you want to learn more about anything I suggest. I respect and value the sources. I do my best to credit properly. I appreciate our ability to share and harmonize together in this Sacred Circle of Life. When my mom died in 2010, I started an effort called "P.A.S. it on." Her initials were P.A.S., and I wanted to pass on her zest and legacy of love for others, nature, and life! I no longer use that name because there was already something like it, yet the intention is still similar. This book feels like that coming to fruition, passing on a love for life and ideas that have been enriching and enlightening to me. I think of it like a nourishing bowl of fruit being shared. Take any of the fruit you like. Leave the rest.

This book is intended to be inclusive and accessible to anyone regardless of cultural backgrounds, religious affiliations or political persuasions. I've collected inspiration from a variety of traditions and sources. If you disagree with an idea, I encourage you to:

1. Consider how and why you accept a particular belief. Notice if it is truly serving your best interest and seems healthy for you and all of creation. If so, then

2. See if you can adapt or revise the idea I share to be more in alignment with your own core values and beliefs or

3. Totally ignore anything I suggest that you don't find worthwhile or in accord with your own deepest truths. I might even disagree with myself by the time you read this!

I am not seeking nor pushing any particular answers to life's great mysteries. Rather, I explore them and experiment with many ideas. Like life, I seem to be full of contradictions and wonder. I'm open to entertaining various questions and ideas. I may change my mind and opinions often. I'm just a girl finding my way in this world. If you find yourself saying, "This girl doesn't know what she's talking about" while reading, you're right! As Aaron Neville sings, "I don't know much..." Rather, I wonder, think, and feel a lot! I tend to dabble in many ideas and rarely adopt any more strictly. It seems to suit my curious, eclectic nature. I think of introductions to various topics like taste testing. Enjoy favorite activities you know you like and sample the others. Many of the suggestions have entire books written about them. There are plenty of resources and references at the end of the book and on the resources webpage for the book.

I use the ideas in this book to cope with life and dance with delight. I have trusted the flow of my voice, vision, and inspiration while writing. I trust my Source. If something comes up more than once, I expect the repetition is valuable. It's amazed me how many times I may need to hear or consider things before I start to understand, see from a fresh perspective, or have a new interpretation. There may be many layers I need to work through. Maybe I need to feel things deep in my bones or allow things to flow through me with physical movement. Sometimes, I need to have a conversation, write, or share ideas to review perceptions. Maybe my brain needs to do some rewiring. I imagine this is true for many of us. I trust messages that may be enriching or enlightening for you to stand out and sing to you. I think of that as a gift being offered. I hope you open the presents! I'm glad to be a messenger and presenter.

I am aware that the experiences I've had are results of the cultures and the environments I've lived in and ideas I've been exposed to. While I sometimes try to imagine myself in someone else's shoes or situation, I realize it's not the same as having those experiences or circumstances. For example, I've found that being a parent is much different than babysitting! I remember when I found out that I was pregnant with twins, which was a huge surprise. I recall thinking, "I don't even really know what to do with one baby much less two at the same time!" My husband's response was much more practical, "Well, you have two boobs." Oh, my! It was more like having two huge water balloons when breastfeeding twins.

I had no idea what it was like to have significantly premature babies and spend three whole months pumping breast milk to tube feed, visiting babies for specific 'touch times' in the hospital, and hoping they would survive and thrive. They probably wouldn't have if we'd lived in some other places. I don't know if it's right or wrong to use technology that way, but I'm glad they are healthy boys now. That experience is one we can't fully fathom without living it, even if we empathize. The same is true for seeing a loved one take their last breath. There are surely situations and circumstances beyond me.

My heart grows heavy thinking of hungry children, abuse, neglect, war zones, addiction, disease, orphans, violence, oppression, and poverty. All of those reasons motivate me to not let myself dwell in despair, depression, or self-pity, especially since I have had a very fortunate life overall. While we all have our own unique journeys, experiences and perspectives, we still share similar core feelings. I hope my offerings may honor and respect all of life. I do not want to take life nor the many blessings and opportunities for granted!

I don't 'have it all figured out.' I'm very sensitive. I am not immune to the weight of the world. I sometimes find my mind in the gutter. I'm not fearless, free of doubts, or without skeptical voices. I've had low self esteem and felt lost and lonely at times. I have blind spots like everyone else. I sometimes feel resistance to living and loving fully and openly. If you don't experience any of that stuff yet somehow ended up with this book, you may not appreciate it. You could pass it on to a library where others may find value within it. I still experience that stuff sometimes. I've retreated from the world in many ways to a sanctuary in the woods. I'm a bit of a hermit and a woodland creature. It's my gentle way of being a rebel and "living on the edge" as Aerosmith sings.

This book is sort of my version of the Zen idea about 'returning to the marketplace' or public area. I'm glad to share ways I've found to cope with and love life, ways I dance in the rain when it comes and even let it cleanse, heal, and nourish me, and ways I dance with delight. This book is about renewal, refreshment, rejuvenation, and rejoicing. It is about leaning in to life even with all of the messes and mysteries. It's about finding the magic within it all.

Writing this book has been such a gift to me. I didn't know I had it in me until I let it flow out! So, I'm willing to promote delight and present this book to the world. I'm grateful to be the messenger. I feel there is so much enriching depth still to explore myself even though I've been doing the D.A.N.C.E. ritual for a while. I recall a suggestion that it's good to write what we most need to hear. That totally applies to this for me! I hope it's worthwhile for you as well.

I don't have any prescriptions for happy pills. Yet, I do think there is potential for nourishing soul food, spirit medicine, and sweetness when we water the seeds of joy and tend to our inner gardens to harvest delight. We can explore the possibilities while tuning in and doing the symbolic dance of life. Approaching some serious or heavy stuff in fun, fulfilling, liberating ways helps me lighten up.

I share from my own healing journey in this book. We each have our own paths to live. I focus on healing, being, and loving myself while respecting life and creation. I take responsibility for myself and recognize that you are responsible for yourself, which I find liberating for both of us. You're free to take your own steps! There are as many ways as there are lives. I hope you enjoy exploring the ideas shared within this book. I applaud you for taking each step, making time to dance with yourself, and finding your own ways to thrive, love, and enjoy. I gladly cheer you on through these pages!

I share a lot about the process of writing the book within it because it relates to the notes step of the D.A.N.C.E. and being the authors who are writing the stories of our own lives as we prefer to live.

My husband and I were watching a hummingbird acting funny one day when I said, "It's doing a little dance!" He said, "for itself?" I said, "Why not? I do!" I hope you enjoy dancing with yourself, too!

May we be blessed with the ability to dance with life, the strength to dance in the rain and bright rainbows after storms in our lives.

Let's liven up and lighten up!

HOW TO USE THIS BOOK

This book is designed to use for a full 30 day moon cycle, which is the original foundation for our current months. You can start at any time of month or phase of the moon. There truly is no time like the present! There is no need to stick strictly to the book's 30 day cycle. It is simply a way to organize the information to share many options while developing a routine and rhythm. The idea is to give it at least one whole 30 day moon cycle to experiment while finding your own preferences and creating a habit. I also just love the notion of dancing with the moon! There are plenty possibilities to keep us dancing for many moons.

In this book, I share several aspects, activities, and alternatives for the letters representing the D.A.N.C.E. ritual on different days. I don't actually try to fit it ALL in at once on any single day! I started with the basics as suggested for each letter, which is still what I do to keep it sweet and simple most days. I've explored several more ideas to expand on it over time. Now, I keep the basic D.A.N.C.E. steps in mind and go with the flow of my energy, needs, desires, inspiration, joys, and available time on any given day. It can take just a few minutes! If you're fortunate to have more time, it can be much longer and so sweet. Anything goes! I don't stress about missing a day, but I do notice. If you want to take a break, go ahead! Distance might let the heart grow fonder. Take as long as you need and give it another go whenever you're ready. Keep it easy and joyful so it's something to look forward to.

We start with super simple and short ways to incorporate the basic activities into the day. Just like swing dancing has a few basic steps that can be built upon to make all sorts of more elaborate fun and fancy dances, there are basic steps for the D.A.N.C.E. ritual that can be experimented with and expanded upon in many enriching ways later. We dive deeper with more options as we go through the full cycle of the book. You can keep it simple by doing the basic steps as covered over the first five days for as long as you wish.

You could read the entire book first to get a preview if you want to choose what to explore when. If you tend to get overwhelmed with information overload, then you can take it one day at a time with me in the order that is presented or you can spend many days on a single step before moving on. Try on different ideas like clothes or dancing shoes. My husband uses the phrase, 'if the shoe fits.' I say if it fits and you like it! I don't enjoy high heels. I prefer bare feet, flip flops, slippers, or boots. If anything feels too tight for your free spirit, you don't need to squeeze into it! If something feels too big, like oversized clown shoes that don't provide enough support or trip you up, leave it behind. Trust what feels like a good fit for you.

The ideas are spread out over different days to give you time to try many things and see what you enjoy without packing too much into any single day. If a specific topic interests you more, you can skip to that day at anytime. Some days have several possible ideas so you can pick and choose what sings to you and leave out any that don't. You might find that you want to go back to some ideas more than once. You may want to skip a day or a few. You could select one suggestion from a page one day and another suggestion from the same page on a different day. Once you've done the basic steps from the first day, you can keep doing that most days if you want. Then, you could use this more like a reference book to invite serendipity and synchronicity to dance with you by choosing a page at random some days. After getting in the groove with the basic steps, you could spread the additional ideas out over 30 weeks, months, seasons, or even years to expand upon the basics. The best way to use this book is to actually use it. So, use it in any way that you enjoy doing so! There are no rules. "Dance to the music" and the rhythm of your own heart and soul. Feel free to skip around if you like, take as long as you like to try all of the various ideas, and repeat the suggestions from the first day anytime you need or want to keep it short, sweet, and simple! You can do your own intuitive D.A.N.C.E. for as many moons as you feel inspired and enjoy it.

These are the basic D.A.N.C.E. steps:

Dance
Affirmations
Notes
Celebration
Embrace

I might do the affirmations and celebration (gratitude) either while still in bed (mentally or aloud) or, most often, aloud while dancing. 'Dancing' can look like stretching, yoga, tapping, tai chi, ballet, salsa dancing, jumping jacks, gymnastics, or any movement, depending on your mood and allotted time. The order of activities represented by the letters doesn't matter. It's the combination that is magical. Having the letters and ideas match with the word D.A.N.C.E. also helps me remember what to do while waking up!

After my mom died, I went through a few years of sleepless nights due to severe insomnia. I've experienced my share of exhaustion. I've felt depressed at times. I still wake up tired sometimes and feeling like a failure before the day even begins. Maybe that's why this ritual is something I appreciate so much. I'm thankful to live my days with brighter eyes more often thanks to getting fresh air and revising the soundtrack in my head, like changing the station or changing my tune, during the morning D.A.N.C.E. time. Now, I'm singing, "turn around, bright eyes" with Bonnie Tyler.

At the time of this writing, I have the full range of motion in my physical body. I share my experiences based on that. My body is less flexible than it once was so I take it a bit slower than I might have when I was a teen. I enjoy stretching. If you're young and in great shape, you might choose to jump right in and bust a move! I'm singing along with Young MC now. Do you know the song? Probably not if you're too young! MC stands for the 'master of ceremonies.' I guess I get to MC this dance party for now.

If you have any injuries or physical disabilities, please consult a physician or take your circumstances into account. You can make adjustments as needed. You can visualize the movement or replace it with sitting meditation if needed. It can be fun to imagine being a porpoise playing in the ocean waves or a seagull gliding with the wind. There are plenty of other ways to participate as well.

If you are going to do the D.A.N.C.E. in the morning and have limited time due to school or work, you could read the information for the following day the night before. That way you can use your time each morning to fully enjoy the D.A.N.C.E! I prefer to do all of the D.A.N.C.E. steps before looking at any kind of computer or phone screen in the morning. It's a great way to tune in to ourselves, our own hopes, loves, and vibrations, first. I can remember way back before having kids when I used to fit in a 90 minute yoga class before going to work in the mornings. I also remember when I had babies to tend to and barely had time to go pee first thing in the morning since they woke up early and hungry! Now, I gladly take 15 minutes to feel fabulous first thing when I can. Some days, I get up too late or have something else that needs attention first. I still like to fit the steps in once I get a chance most days, and I love when I can give it even more time. You could try different times of day to see what you prefer. It's also a great way to tune in to your own rhythm after school or work. Anytime you can is a good time to loosen up, liven up, and lighten up with a little D.A.N.C.E!

You can use #DanceWithDelight to share on social media and join a worldwide dance party/book club online from the resources link.

DAY 1

DO A LITTLE DANCE, BASIC STEPS

It feels important to emphasize the idea of dancing like no one is watching, especially while first diving in to this intuitive dancing ritual and finding your own rhythm. If possible, choose a place that you truly won't have anyone else watching in the beginning. Privacy allows us to be free from the concerns of what anyone else might think! That freedom is a necessary basic step to getting in tune with our own natural rhythms and inner wisdom. It's fun to do a little "dancing with myself" as Billy Idol sings. Later, you can dance in public or social settings and notice how it impacts your flow.

Let's start with a short, soft, slow dance to tune in. I rarely have music playing when doing the D.A.N.C.E. ritual and going through the activities for the letters. I find it's easier to tune in to my own rhythm without music. I'm also able to focus more on affirmations and celebration while dancing. I love to dance with music at other times, especially my husband's acoustic guitar. You could try with or without music on different days to see what you prefer.

Here are the basic steps to remember:

Dance
Affirmations
Notes
Celebration
Embrace

For this first day, I encourage you to start slow and see where your natural rhythm leads. Start with a few big, deep breaths. Please do whatever feels good with your body as you do so. I enjoy opening my arms up wide towards the sky, either making a letter Y or like open wings. The simple act of opening our arms wide to greet the day can feel so good! It can even be done while getting out of bed.

As I start the dance with arms wide open, I can feel my head and heart opening as well. Then, I bring the arms back in over the heart center as if gathering pure energy and bringing it in to the heart. I open the arms back up again and go back and forth repeating the motion with each inhale and exhale a few more times. I often find myself greeting the day with "Good Morning, Life," and "Good Morning, Body" or singing something like, "I greet this world with arms wide open" from a song I love by the band Creed.

As in music, there is a special role for rest in our lives. If you're starting this on a waning moon or you've been sick or you're a woman and choosing to start this during your monthly cycle, it's especially worthwhile to respect the role of rest and allow yourself to do so if needed. On days when I need to rest, I may simply greet the day with arms wide open. Then, close my arms around myself in a loving embrace.

If feeling up for it, I may also stretch a little. I usually bend forward to touch the ground to get the blood flowing and feel in to my body while stretching. While bending down, I let my hands, arms, and head softly and slowly sway back and forth. I often bend my knees and move hips side to side to feel a stretch in my hips, back, and legs. It's like giving my body a massage with the movement.

If you're feeling more energetic as you start moving, go with it and dance in whatever way feels great! This is time for intuitive dancing so do any movement you are inspired to do. It can look more like stretching or yoga. It can be like ballet, tap dancing, breakdancing, line dancing, zumba, ballroom dancing or dirty dancing!

Both girls and guys can dance! Look at Michael Jackson. Regardless of anything else, that man could dance! I used to love the *Breakin'* movies in the 80's with Ozone and Turbo. I also remember those MC Hammer pants. Patrick Swayze was a cool dirty dancing dude. Channing Tatum has some moves, too! I've seen many men who are better dancers than me. It doesn't matter how great we are at dancing anyway! This isn't like the old *American Bandstand* show. It isn't a performance for anyone else. It's about what we enjoy! Maybe this book came through me instead of an *American Idol* so I could be an example of an average, everyday, phenomenal person dancing with delight and letting my heart sing. So can you!

If the idea of 'dancing' just doesn't appeal to you, then you can replace that step with any other kind of intuitive movement. You can do karate kicks or cartwheels if you feel like it. You could make some music like my husband prefers to do instead. You can even change the acronym. You could use the word Declarations for the letter D to take the place of affirmations and use the word Actions for the letter A to represent any type of movement if you prefer.

Keeping it simple today, you can choose one easy affirmation statement that feels both good and true to you and something to celebrate while stretching or dancing. For example, I often say, "I am grateful for this strong, flexible body. I am full of life and love."

This can be done in just ten minutes with a quick stretch if time is short. If you have more time and feel inspired, you can dance for as long as you have the energy. I like alliteration so I like the sound of "15 minutes to feel fabulous!" It could be 5, 15, or 40 minutes to feel fabulous depending on the day for me. If you are able to some days, it's great to keep moving for long enough to get your heart drumming and have your body release some feel good endorphins. If weather permits, it's also refreshing to do your dance outside. You can continue saying what you are celebrating and affirmations for the duration of your dance or you can focus your full attention on enjoying the movement. This is your dance and anything goes!

If you have a shorter timeframe, only spend a couple of minutes dancing or moving to loosen up. Then, keep your notes short by writing a single affirmation and celebration note or skip the notes. Even just five minutes to do the D.A.N.C.E. can help us be more present and enjoy feeling fabulous, especially if body, mind, and spirit associate the ritual steps with that feeling from other times.

You can choose affirmations and celebration while you are dancing or wait until taking notes instead of thinking about that while doing your movement if you prefer. I think both writing and movement may increase the influence of our words. If you have more time, you can write anything you want for as long as you like in your notes. Taking that time while writing to let your thoughts flow freely and unedited onto a page can help to focus and cleanse the mind. It can also help create new thought patterns.

You can end this day's dance with a lovely embrace. Wrap your arms around yourself for a big self love hug!

Let's join KC and the Sunshine band to "do a little D.A.N.C.E.," make a lot of love, and lighten up today. Enjoy!

Dance
Affirmations
Notes
Celebration
Embrace

Remember, you can do as much or as little as you choose. You can repeat the suggestions from this day for a week, a month or a year. The basic steps are the ones I do most days. The additional options are great ways to explore if you have the inclination. They're not necessary for the ritual to have an enriching presence in your life! If you ever feel like adding more is too much, repeat the suggestions from today instead. Give yourself 15 minutes to feel fabulous most days. Keep it simple instead of quitting so soon. Make it your own!

DAY 2

AFFIRMATIONS, TRUST YOUR SONG

"May my words be rooted in loving kindness. I trust my pure voice to flow forth with ease, grace, joy, reverence, and inspiration." That is my affirmation and prayer while typing this!

I've included Affirmations as one of the basic daily D.A.N.C.E. steps because we have the ability to imagine, because we all have a sort of soundtrack playing in our heads, and because our thoughts, words, prayers, and lyrics have power. Many of us are constantly affirming something whether we intend to or not.

What is the soundtrack of your life?

I came across that idea in the novel *Sing You Home* by Jodi Picoult shortly after my mom died. I realized that I had literally used a soundtrack for my mom's life with the video that I made for her memorial celebrations. Before she died, my mom requested one specific song to be played as she shared with us how she wanted to have celebrations in her memory rather than a funeral (on special dates she chose at two different places she loved). As I prepared a video slideshow, I arranged it to play with the song she requested, "Our House" by Crosby, Stills, and Nash, along with more songs that made me think of her. Now, I'm attentive to the soundtrack for my own life, from popular songs and from my own inner voice.

Before choosing affirmations, it helps to listen and tune in.

What lyrics are already playing, often on repeat, in our heads? Who is the DJ selecting the playlist? Who is writing the songs? Inner critic or inner lover? What are the songs affirming? Are the lyrics from our own intuition, our inner wisdom? To me, intuition has a lot to do with knowing and trusting our selves! Do you know what makes your heart sing? Do you trust your instincts and desires? Do you trust your own true nature? These are questions I have been asking myself. Trust has been a big topic and challenge in my life.

Now, I'm leaning in to trust myself and life more.

When choosing affirmations, I encourage you to consider what makes you smile, what warms your heart, what do you appreciate, what do you love, and what have you wished for. The first time I tried using affirmations many years ago, I borrowed other people's affirmations or aligned my own affirmations with what I thought I 'should' want, be, or do. I see now that I didn't believe nor truly trust many of those early affirmations. I often felt longing or doubt when saying them. It has made a difference for me to explore my own head and heart, to ask myself questions about how I prefer to feel and live right here and now, and to trust what I hear my own inner compass pointing towards. Now, I choose affirmations that make me feel both honest and good. I feel good when both my heart and my head are in harmony.

As part of tuning in and learning to harmonize, I consider whether my affirmations are genuinely coming more from a voice of love or a voice of fear. I'm glad that my friend, Corinne Zupko, author of *From Anxiety To Love*, recently reminded me to notice which voice is doing the speaking or writing the songs! For example, if I say: "I am wealthy. I can easily afford to pay all of my bills and give to charity and have a savings net." I can sense that those words are partly addressing my fears of the opposite. I can almost hear the echoes of fear as back-up singers! As a mother, I've noticed that the voices of fear and love sometimes sound similar or seem to exist at the same time. Some of my fears seem to be rooted in love.

Still, I feel that I can lean more towards love that feels less fearful and more delightful! Maybe I can even serenade my ego guardian with wonder, grace, reverence, and joy filled love songs.

When I say: "I am wellthy (I spell it that way purposely). I love the variety in my life. I love tasting so many different kinds of fruit! I am full of love and life. I trust my head, my heart, my hands, and the magic of the Multiverse. I am grateful and generous. I am open, willing, and able to let love and life flow through me with ease. I love feeling and sharing and enjoying the beauty and magic and sweetness all around me and within me. I love thriving!" These words feel like I'm focusing more on my blessings, hopes, loves, joys, excitement, and opportunities. It also feels like I am leaving plenty of room for Divine guidance or flow regarding the details.

Do your affirmations make you smile? Are both your head and your heart singing in harmony? Is your whole body and spirit saying a big Holy YES?! That's my flip side of heck no!

I've learned to trick my inner skeptic if I hear a part of me react to my affirmations with a doubtful, "Yeah, Right." Do you know the song "Oh Yeah" by Yello? It's in the movie *Ferris Bueller.* I love the song! It makes me smile and lighten up. I love the deep voice and the fun sounds. If you don't know the song, I invite you to listen to it for the full effect. Now, when I hear a cynical "Yeah, Right" pop into my head doubting something my heart is affirming, I revise it. I start singing a deep, "Oh Yeah... Beautiful!"

I immediately feel a shift in my entire energy! My head starts to sing along with my heart because it's too fun to resist. The resistance shifts to wide open and welcoming receptivity! I might throw my arms open wide like a big capital letter Y for Yes! My heart vibes rumble, "Oh Yeah!" My head even starts shaking an affirmative, "Yes." I think Liz Gilbert would be proud of my inner trickster. She shares about the role of a trickster in her book called *Big Magic.* Oh Yeah, I feel the magic!

Now, speaking or singing my affirmations aloud while dancing fans the flames of life sparkling in my eyes and brings a soft smile to my soul. I'm learning to live in love and enjoy the dance. While you are welcome to borrow any affirmations I share in examples, especially if they warm your heart, I hope you will also enjoy creating your own so you may sing your own sweet songs! (And please ignore any affirmations I share that do not fully resonate with you!)

Personally, I don't use a list of written affirmations to read, recall, or recite what I want to say. Yet, I often write them in my notes during or after the daily D.A.N.C.E. time. I prefer to say them in the present tense and choose and feel them in the present. I simply let whatever comes to my head AND heart flow. I usually say them out loud while dancing (or stretching or resting) in the moment that I'm doing my daily D.A.N.C.E. ritual.

Some days, my voice may be a whisper. Sometimes, I might stay silent and say them to myself in my head. Other times, I sing them loud and clear or soft and sweet. Trust your instincts at the time.

Have the audacity, by which I mean both courage and honesty combined, to declare and affirm how you really prefer to feel and live. I use the word 'prefer' rather than 'want' or 'need' on purpose. Notice the soundtrack that is playing in your life and choose what you are affirming for yourself. Be your own DJ and songwriter.

Though I usually don't have any music with me, I do sometimes end up with songs playing in my head. I might find myself singing along with Bob Marley saying, "Sing your sweet song... a melody pure true" or with U2 singing "It's a beautiful day..."

Sometimes, I might not love all of the lyrics that pop into my head along with a particular song. In those cases, I change the lyrics! I'll replace some words to make new lyrics that are more in tune with my own hopes. Then, I start singing that instead. For example, the song 'Last Dance' by Donna Summer came into my head one day.

My head is full of random lyrics! I wasn't feeling in the mood for the lyrics as they really go, yet the tune was stuck on repeat. So, I made up new lyrics that went well enough with the tune and started singing that to myself instead: "This dance... is a great chance... for love." I've done the same thing with the song 'Bad Moon Rising' by Creedence Clearwater Revival in my head. I revised the lyrics to sing to myself, "There's a full moon on the rise" instead. I change the song Mick Jagger sings about satisfaction to say YES to satisfaction! Even subtle changes can impact how the energy of the words influences us. I've started singing "this lovely light of mine" rather than "this little light of mine" because I'd rather not focus on the size. I am accepting and embracing my "muchness," as the Mad Hatter calls it in *Alice in Wonderland!*

I used to mumble and be embarrassed if I didn't know all of the correct lyrics when singing along in the car with other people. Now, I love that I let my own heart sing! I think this revising of popular song lyrics is a healthy habit to practice so that we can also apply it to other thoughts in our heads that we may have inherited or adopted, yet prefer to change. This is another way we can utilize affirmations to speak lovingly and compassionately to ourselves. Revise any thoughts that play on repeat in your head if necessary!

If I'm too distracted or at a loss with my own words some days for affirmations, then I may use a song that lifts my spirits instead. I love "Glorious" by MaMuse. So, I might sing that to myself while dancing, "Oh, what a day... Glorious!" I also enjoy starting the day with the chorus from "Feeling Good" as sung by Nina Simone.

I tend to combine my affirmations and grateful celebration. I think of it as a kind of prayer or offering blessings. I used to start my day with a morning blessing before I started using the D.A.N.C.E. acronym. I was inspired by the way John O'Donohue describes blessings in his book, *To Bless the Space Between Us*, to create and memorize my own daily blessing. It grew and evolved over time. I probably have a longer version saved in a notebook somewhere.

This is what I said daily, still remember, and still say for all of us:

> May we thrive
> true, open, and free,
> happy and healthy
> in harmony.

I combined words my family and I chose that year with a few more to create it. My words were thrive and harmony, my husband's was true, and my boys chose happy and healthy. You could think of affirmations as declarations, prayers, blessings or simple reminders. I might say, "I am blessed with each breath. I feel the flow of life in me. I am part of a whole wonderful world." I enjoy singing along with Israel Kamakawiwo'ole, "and I think to myself... what a wonderful world." May we bless the space within and all around us.

Now, I also love taking dance breaks for the simple act of dancing without the rest of the ritual. My subconscious might associate the affirmations, gratitude, energy, and loving embraces with dancing at any time of day since the ritual is a habit. This makes it even more fun and uplifting to dance! Trust what brings you true, pure joy.

As you do your D.A.N.C.E. today, choose an affirmation that feels good and lights you up! Say it (or sing it!) while Dancing, Affirm it, write it in your Notes, Celebrate your sweet song, and give yourself a loving Embrace. Let Your Heart Sing! Dance with Delight!

> **D**ance
> **A**ffirmations
> **N**otes
> **C**elebration
> **E**mbrace

You can share affirmations or favorite songs that liven you up, on social media with #DanceWithDelight. If you prefer to be a private dancer, that's cool, too! Let your lovely light shine your way!

DAY 3

NOTES, LISTEN TO YOUR LIFE

I encourage you to keep a journal as part of the daily D.A.N.C.E. The N stands for Notes. The origin for the word journal is based on the old French word jornel meaning "what takes place daily." While researching it, there was a deeper Latin root that meant "to shine." I love the idea of shining daily and taking notice of what lights us up, both inside and out, during our days.

I've kept some sort of journal (or many journals at the same time!) throughout my life. I've found that the act of writing whatever is in our heads and hearts at a given time can enable us to listen more deeply to our lives and get in touch with our inner guidance and wisdom. It also helps me to clean out my often overflowing head! As Dave Matthews sings, "my head won't leave my head alone."

I admit this step can be time consuming. It's great when we can allow plenty of time to write for as long as a stream of thoughts is flowing. Yet, we can still take very quick notes when needed. Some days, I start with this step, especially if I've had some dreams that I want to make note of before I forget or have some ideas that came to me in the night that I want to jot down. Sometimes, my notes may look more like a to do list. Sometimes, I do morning gratitude pages because it feels so good to start my days with appreciation. Sometimes, I write love letters. Most often, I'll write some of the affirmations that come out while dancing. I've also taken many notes for this book as ideas came to me during my dance time!

Absolutely anything goes for your notes, any number of words and pages, any length of time, and any ideas, joys, wild wishes, prayers, quotes, lyrics, one word to focus on, scribbles, doodles, venting, observations, declarations, conversations, jokes, or questions that come to mind! My notes are a marvelous mess of magic, medicine, messages, and "things that make me go hmmm" like noticing the words mess and ages are in messages! I like word wizardry, wonder, inquisitive writing, love notes, and gladness. Our journals can help us be our own best friends, magic mirrors, investigators, mentors, memory keepers, lovers, and cheerleaders on our journeys.

If I don't do notes because time is short, I may take notes later. It doesn't need to happen the same way every day. As with each part of the D.A.N.C.E., do what works best for you at the time. Skip it anytime you want to. Let it support you rather than pressure you!

Though I love many kinds of journals, I tend to use inexpensive notebooks that I can scribble in, tear pages from, write easy, big, and plenty in for this. I've enjoyed inspiration and encouragement from *The Artist's Way* by Julia Cameron, *Writing Down the Bones* by Natalie Goldberg, *Poem Crazy* by Susan Wooldridge, *Writing Down Your Soul* by Janet Conner, and *Journalution* by Sandy Grason.

I especially love including affirmations in my notes because writing seems to help our brains revise and retain the information better. I prefer the voice in my head to be focusing more on what I choose to affirm, attract, and celebrate. This also encourages me to take action in alignment with those preferences.

As you do your D.A.N.C.E. today, choose an affirmation(s) that feels good! Say it while Dancing, Affirm it, write anything you like in your Notes, Celebrate, and give yourself a big loving Embrace.

Notice how it feels to Dance with Delight. Let Your Heart Sing!

Refresher: **D**ance, **A**ffirmations, **N**otes, **C**elebration, **E**mbrace

DAY 4

CELEBRATION, FEELING GRATEFUL JOY

You are invited to a sweet celebration in honor of your life each and every day! To me, choosing and celebrating joy are part of falling in love with life. I have recognized over the past few years that I often used to feel guilty for experiencing joy. I don't deny the pain in the world or in our own lives, yet it feels encouraging and healthy to give more attention to joy. I've kept a gratitude journal off and on for about two decades. It has been challenging at times to think of something to be thankful for, such as when my mom was diagnosed with ovarian cancer in 2008 and left her body 19 months later. Still, I'm willing to choose and celebrate joy as often as I can. From the warmth of the winter sunshine to the hugs with my children before bedtime to the glistening dew drops or ice crystals sparkling in the morning, I want to be present and notice the many big and little joys and gifts that make life wonderful.

I wish to acknowledge and remind myself that we have choices, even amidst all of the drama, striving, suffering, and circumstances often beyond our control. We can choose to 'open' the gifts of joy that can be found right here and now. It doesn't mean that we won't also feel worry, grief, frustration, sadness, etc.

While writing this book, my father-in-law had a heart attack and was in the hospital. We visited him in the hospital. We helped out with chores at their home. My husband, kids, and I also went for walks together outside. We enjoyed strawberry crepes for dessert.

We sat on a swing in our backyard watching the birds. We noticed spring blooms. It was healthy for us to get fresh air and surround ourselves with natural wonder and beauty. We also sat together inside around a fire in the woodstove. We talked and shared hugs all while still concerned and waiting for news from the hospital.

Admittedly, it's harder to do that kind of thing if you're the one in the hospital! Yet, I heard that my father-in-law made an effort to find a window where he could see the open sky. I remember my mom's eyes lighting up when her grandkids came to see her in the hospital, even when she was in severe pain after her surgeries. I remember her asking my boys to climb into her hospice bed with her for hugs just a few days before she died. I'm thankful for her example of leaning in to joyful love through it all! I think having experiences like those may make me appreciate being able to take a clear deep breath when I can or smell the roses even more.

Tuning in and being aware of all the different feelings we have is part of using our intuition and instincts and how we live. Still, I prefer to notice joy, to lean in to the sweetness in life, to celebrate it and share it often. I like to sing, "I wanna spread joy over this land" with Patti Casey or "Joy to the World" by Three Dog Night.

Each day during my D.A.N.C.E., I give thanks and celebrate some sweet, simple joys, such as watching the moon rise, or sharing a juicy, delicious and nourishing harvest of fruit with my family. I almost always feel blessed in the present moment when I focus on celebrating without feeling obligated to be grateful. I've adapted these words for blessings: presentce, meaning the gifts of now, and blissings, meaning moments of joy! I often finish my D.A.N.C.E. feeling and declaring, "I'm gifted and blessed here and now!" I sing my own version of the Jesus Jones song, "right here, right now" waking up from history and watching the world with all its mystery.

What can you celebrate during your D.A.N.C.E. today? Blessed Be!

Refresher: **D**ance, **A**ffirmations, **N**otes, **C**elebration, **E**mbrace

DAY 5

EMBRACE YOUR WHOLE SELF AND LIFE

This D.A.N.C.E. step is all about giving yourself some love, sweet love. If this doesn't come easy for you at first, I hope you will give it a try every day for the rest of this full length moon cycle. It didn't always come easy to me. Yet, it has become such a powerful gift to myself. Learning to love myself has had an amazing influence on many areas of my life, including my ability to listen to my intuition, be honest with myself, trust myself, be creative, feel more alive, and be genuinely encouraging, compassionate, accepting, generous, and kind to others. I hope you find it to be a blessing as well.

Most days, usually after the other D.A.N.C.E. steps, I end the ritual with a big embrace! Open your arms wide. Then, wrap each hand around the opposite shoulder to give yourself a huge hug. You can close your eyes and take a few deep breaths while holding yourself in a loving embrace.

When I have time and feel a need for extra TLC (total loving care), I'll mentally send love and gratitude to each cell in my body. When I first started adding movement to my morning spiritual practice, I was having some health issues and often in physical pain. It actually hurt to sit down for too long at a time. So, I started moving and stretching more instead of being still for as long during the time I usually set aside for meditation. Starting to move and stretch during meditation time inspired me to tune in to my body more. I started slow dancing because it helped relieve the pain and felt good!

To send love and gratitude to each cell in my body, I often start with my feet and work my way slowly all the way up to the top of my head. I might even name specific organs and give thanks for the job they do. For example, "I love these two feet. I'm so thankful for all of the steps I've taken and how well these feet carry me through this journey. I send love to my heart. I'm grateful for the healthy flow my heart provides. I love my hands. I'm so glad that I'm able to hug and nurture and create and give and receive. I'm grateful for every single healthy cell in my body." If I'm having any pain due to back aches, fibroids, cramps, headaches, aging knees, tension, a twisted ankle, or whatever else, I send extra love to those areas along with well wishes. It feels much better than complaining!

I'll wonder what my body may need in order to be well. I am gentle with my body the same way I would be with anyone else in pain. I might mentally release past injuries and invite healing. As I was writing this, I fell while climbing over a fence on our homestead. I bruised my leg and slightly twisted my ankle. I thought, "I didn't mean to end up with a twisted ankle when I wrote about possibly having one!" Was it the law of attraction or power of suggestion? Another reason to choose loving thoughts for our body rather than complain about a pain in the neck! I slowed down during my dance for a while. Still, I was thankful my body can heal pretty well from that sort of thing and how amazing it is. I was also glad that I still go exploring in the woods and climbing over fences in my forties!

I've come to think of a body as a sensual gift, a kind of temple and vessel. I've playfully thought of it as my ATV, or all terrain vehicle, for exploring the world. Though I no longer let it define me or derive my beauty from it, I do appreciate it. I am also the breath, water, wonder, spirit, joy and love that flow through my body.

I once heard someone refer to aging as "saging" like becoming a wise sage. Now, I'm able to see the beauty at every age in others, especially my Grammie who is in her 90's. I love seeing the Delight in her eyes when we visit with her. I love her giggles. I was blessed to find an elegant book of *Wise Women* by Joyce Tenneson years ago. She captures and shares the beauty of several women over 70 years old through her photographs in the book. I'm trying to see the deep, pure beauty in myself as I age also. I've earned more than a few gray hairs. I prefer to be "saging" (not to be confused with sagging!) gracefully and playfully, in spite of physical stuff I could dwell on. My mom was 62 when she died. Old age isn't guaranteed. I've learned to appreciate that each year we are blessed with love and laughter is a gift. I'm able to truly celebrate my birthdays as the candles grow in number and the light gets brighter.

Some days, I simply say a few words of kindness instead of more thorough attention to parts of my body during the embrace. For example, "I love, accept, and trust my whole self, my entire body, my curves and my edges, my imperfections, my shadow, my inner sparkling sunshine, my whole sweet silly sacred spirit." I forgive myself if I need to. I might give myself a kiss on the hand as well.

I didn't always have this loving relationship with my body. As a teen, I nearly tried to starve myself to be thin. I don't think the diet Mountain Dew was a very healthy liquid diet! I may be considered overweight by others now. Yet, I feel strong and capable of hiking and caring for myself and others and enjoying life. I don't bleach my teeth so I have felt insecure about my smile sometimes. I had to forgive my womb for not being able to keep my twin boys safely inside until the due date. My water broke and they were rushed out of me with an emergency c-section. They had to be resuscitated and on life support in the hospital for the remaining three months they should have been in my body. They had bleeding in the brain that could have caused brain damage. One had a collapsed lung. It was scary stuff! Thankfully, they are thriving thirteen year old boys as I write this. I grieved for the way I would have preferred giving birth to be. I've forgiven my body and myself for the way it was.

I no longer say I hate my body from my bellybutton to my knees. It may be because my body has survived so much, including abuse from others and me, and continues to carry me through each day. It may be because I made a decision to love it and stop comparing myself to magazines or that I witnessed my mom's body change from cancer or saw my boys developing in neo-natal intensive care. I've learned that wellness and beauty are so much more than skin deep. I'm experimenting with loving my body instead of dieting. I'm feeding myself love and appreciation rather than criticism! I think I may just get healthier and lovelier as a result. Now, I can say, "I love this strong, soft, sensual body" and I mean it!

Learning to treat myself like I want to be treated by a lover or best friend has helped to heal my heart. Looking myself in the mirror and saying whatever it is I've longed to hear has both lifted my own spirit and enabled me to have healthier relationships with loved ones. I no longer get disappointed wishing someone else would fulfill that need for me. I give myself love. I started greeting myself in the mirror with, "Good Morning, Beautiful" a few years ago. I was inspired by a country song's lyrics and wished to be greeted that way in the morning myself. I finally fulfilled my own wish!

Sometimes, I say, "I see the sweet stardust sparkling in those eyes," with a soft smile while looking into my own eyes in my reflection. I started doing that before I came across suggestions from Louise Hay about "mirror work." I've since learned it's a practice many people have found valuable and healing. You can embrace yourself in front of the mirror for this step and smile at yourself. You could look yourself in the eyes while saying affirmations.

I might spend several minutes on this step if giving extra attention to my body as described earlier. Usually, I just take a few seconds for a huge hug after dancing. It's totally up to you based on what you are able to do and feel you need to do on any given day.

I hope you can see the true beauty sparkling within you when you look in the mirror. Enjoy an Embrace in your D.A.N.C.E. today!

Refresher: **D**ance, **A**ffirmations, **N**otes, **C**elebration, **E**mbrace

DAY 6

DREAM ON, DANCE FOR THE YEARS

Another option for the letter D is Dream. This is a great option to do on any days you feel a need to rest. It can also be incorporated into affirmations or notes on days you have the energy to Dance!

Dream can mean daydreaming about your hopes, affirmations, and visions. I love the idea of daydreaming as in living our dreams daily! Alternatively, you can consider any dreams you had when you were sleeping. You could take notes about anything interesting you recall from those dreams in your journal.

When I say the words, "Dream On," I start singing the Aerosmith song. I often rearrange it or add my own lyrics. The song talks about laughter and tears, singing together, and living for both the years and for today. It makes me think about hope, presence, and celebration. I think this D.A.N.C.E. ritual is about all of that.

I think of lyrics from a children's song, "Life is but a dream." I've wondered if life is all a dream. I've also heard others discuss it. Yet, if people treat it as merely a dream or a video game, we might think it doesn't matter if we harm others, ourselves, or the planet. I sense how it could be unhealthy. *The Matrix* movie came to mind. I was surprised to find that the origin and meaning of matrix is mother's womb. That gives me a fresh view of creation as a nourishing place to grow, develop, and thrive. So, I'm leaning in to life even if it's a dream. I think about the idea of lucid dreaming while living.

Lyrics from a song my husband wrote also come to mind, "Are you awake in the dream?" I prefer to be awake and alive in the present moment. I admit I'm currently in no rush to leave the dream, or my body, even if the dream ends in pure bliss and love. So, I appreciate my body as a sacred vessel to explore and enjoy a dreamy world.

However, there have been times in my past when I thought that I'd gladly leave my body and this world behind. I was in a hospital for a mild suicide threat as a teen. I took some pills before I chickened out because I wasn't that serious. I still had to be treated with some disgusting tar like stuff to get them out of my system. There have been times when my imagination, paranoia, and worry have created nightmares I was living in my head. I have struggled with pressure, suffering, and horror in the world. I've seen many movies and heard dooms day broadcasts. I've since decided that I do not want to live out my fears if I don't have to, not even in my head!

When my babies were born and in the neo-natal intensive care unit on life support, the doctors were not optimistic. I remember one of the doctors coming into the room where I was recovering from surgery and telling my husband and me that our babies were "very sick." I instinctively and immediately refused to accept or affirm that! In my momma bear eyes, my babies were born early and still developing, not sick. I was not willing to give that bad dream room to grow! Even while I was in a fog of pain and concern, something deep in me took over and affirmed they were strong. We chose family names that had to do with strength and being gifts honoring God, which I think of as honoring Life and Creation. While I was stuck in my own hospital bed, I was blessed with a deep calmness I can't explain and a knowing that they were going to be okay. Still, it was hard to keep the faith sometimes over the next three months!

I had not yet learned the term "pronoia" to refer to the opposite of paranoia and to assume that life prefers to bless us. Now, if my head starts to create nightmares, I try to use my imagination to envision sweeter dreams instead. I'd rather be a delightful dreamer.

The memory of the hospital doctor makes me think about how our dreams, words, and affirmations can also influence others. When I hear about people going through challenging times, I pray for them to be held in strength, love, and grace, not pity. I don't want to affirm "poor person" or dream the worst for them! Even if tough stuff happens, I try not to add to it nor live more of it in my head.

The song "Imagine" by John Lennon comes to mind about being a dreamer. That song also reminds me affirmations and celebrations can be much broader than about our individual lives, families, and local communities. It makes me think of considering our actions and impact for the whole world and the next seven generations. I dream of a world thriving in harmony. I'm not the only one.

What are your dreams for the world and for posterity? Imagining like Lennon and adding dreams to my affirmations and celebration, I might say: "I see the beauty around me. I'm grateful, kind, and generous. I gladly let love flow through me. I look for and reflect the divine spark in the eyes of others. I enjoy sharing stories with people around the world and learning about various cultures. I'm glad we can encourage and empower one another. I'm grateful for this amazing planet. I gladly share this breath with the trees, birds, animals, and humanity. I am part of this marvelous wholeness."

When thinking about dreams, I also think of the *I Have a Dream* speech by Martin Luther King, Jr. about civil rights.

You can fill in the blank after "I have a dream..." or sing the song by Moody Blues as "Once upon a time in my wildest dreams..." while taking notes and dancing today. Dream with Delight!

Refresher: **D**ance, **A**ffirmations, **N**otes, **C**elebration, **E**mbrace

If the suggestions on any given day don't interest you, simply skip that and do the basic steps as suggested on the first day instead.

DAY 7

AUTHENTICITY, ACTING, ANIMAL SPIRIT

The letter A can also stand for Authenticity. When choosing and creating our affirmations, it is important that they feel honest and valuable to us. Yet, this doesn't mean that we don't also share the same language with some others. I think when a particular painting or quote or song speaks to you, it is often because it is speaking a similar language to your own authentic voice. Hence, we can tune in to our own truths while also harmonizing with kindred spirits.

Have you ever read something and thought, "That's what I keep saying" or wish that you had said it? Maybe that is one way we can listen to our hearts with the help of others. It happens to me more and more often as I follow my genuine curiosity and interests. It even happened a few times while writing this book! Thankfully, it mostly occurred after I had written the content for the first draft. While in the car listening to *Rise Sister Rise* by Rebecca Campbell, I heard some things similar to what I had written a few days before. I could have let that fill me with doubt about whether I should also share. Instead, I've noticed that a source of life and wisdom can flow through many different messengers for different people or different times. I'm glad to know that there are kindred spirits out there sharing similar vibes!

I once heard someone refer to the idea of "original" as being close to or in alignment with our Source/Origin. I love that perspective. It even seems to emphasize cooperation rather than competition to me. I don't remember where I heard it. I share it to state that being authentic doesn't mean we have to try to be different or unique. Sharing similar languages, along with similar hopes and loves, helps us to connect, relate, cooperate and harmonize with each other.

That said, we don't need to try to be more alike others either!

I remember being on vacation with my family in Maine. We were fortunate to rent a home on the water with a view of Acadia National Park. My boys enjoyed exploring the interesting house and decor while we were getting settled. Later, we were on the screen porch together having dinner when my son said, "This house was made by weirdos for weirdos. Luckily for us, we are weirdos!" As we laughed, he went on to say, "I mean face it. We homeschool, Dad works from home…" I love that he was very comfortable with our lifestyle choices as he explained it. Though, he does often remind me that teachers in a 'real school' wouldn't be so distracting by spontaneously singing and dancing in the class when he's doing his school work. If I see a blue bird outside the window, I'll likely bust out singing, "Zip-a-Dee-Doo-Dah." It's a song from an old Disney movie if you don't know it.

We went to another little house further up the coast for a few nights after that. Guess what book my husband found on the end table! It was even one I had in my wish list to eventually purchase. The title was *Blessed are the Weird* by Jacob Nordby.

So, whether you focus on what you have in common with others or notice how you make less popular choices, the point is to tune in to what is genuine and authentic for you. "Be just who you are" as Michael Franti sings about in, "Let It Go." Let your heart sing!

Another way to consider whether we are acting, speaking, and being authentic is to ask ourselves if we would do or say the same thing if no one else was watching or listening? I've noticed this sometimes has a big affect on me. Some people seem to bring out the best in me; others not so much. While there are valid reasons for what is socially acceptable behavior, it may be worthwhile to consider how external factors and other witnesses influence our behavior. We can ask ourselves, "whose voice do we hear?" when a thought comes to mind. Is it ours or could it be a parent, teacher, or preacher we inherited an idea from? In addition to becoming more aware of the sources of our thoughts, taking notes and free writing in our journals is another way to explore our truest selves.

I've gone through many layers of healing regarding my body image and value. When I was fourteen and a size 4/6, I was forced to get on a scale to see my weight. When I tried to get away, my arm was accidentally slammed in a door and my wrist was fractured. I'm not wasting energy pointing fingers. The person acted out of culturally inherited concerns. I can imagine the regret after the situation got out of control and the accident. Others involved don't even recall it the same way I do. I'm trying to gracefully break a chain of learned values and fears. My mom's unconditional love definitely helped!

Have you ever felt like you're being poked, prodded, examined and interrogated by people trying to weigh or diagnose you? I had a job as an actress once, though not a typical one. I was a pretend patient for a medical school that gave us parts to memorize. The students were tested by physically examining us and asking questions to get a diagnosis. It was video recorded to be reviewed and graded. Do you have your part memorized? Did you choose it? You get to have input regarding your part in this play called life!

We might notice how we are acting or not acting in tune with our own heart and soul by acting out a particular role and pretending with purpose. Did you have a favorite thing you liked to act out and pretend to be as a kid? When I was in elementary school, I used to love to use my back porch as a stage while pretending to be Madonna singing and dancing to "Lucky Star." I still love to sing and dance! While writing this book, I had a vision of being on stage singing and dancing again in a way I had never before imagined. I was sharing the ideas from this book with an appreciative audience. It was such a great vision that I fully acted it out the next day on my back porch! I added some of the ideas to the book afterwards.

Is there anything you'd like to try on by acting? You might find that some aspect of your most authentic self can communicate with you that way. Choose a part for yourself and Act 'as if.' What if... I was a writer, inventor, nurse, clown, fill in the blank for yourself?

You can also get more in touch with your authentic core by acting out an animal spirit. For example, I recently spread my arms out wide like wings and imagined myself flying like a bird while I was walking down our long gravel driveway to the mailbox. I might've been singing, "it's time for me to fly." It's even more fun on windy days with my eyes closed! I thought of pelicans I loved watching when I lived in the Florida Keys. I thought about how they are capable of going with the flow when flying and swimming. I think they look sort of silly, yet also embody such grace. I wondered if I might have such a healthy balance with my own silly side and grace.

If you are drawn to a particular animal, you could consider how it might relate to your authenticity. I've even howled at the moon before. It felt good and relieving! Do you know the song by The Script, "I'd howl at the moon," to sing along? I also like one by Aurora singing, "I'm running with the wolves tonight." You could have fun embodying an animal essence in your dance.

Now, choose how you want to explore authenticity today. Let your "true colors shine" like Cyndi Lauper. You could add some kind of acting to your Dance movement, focus on speaking truthfully for your Affirmations, write about any thoughts that these ideas have prompted in your Notes, choose something genuine about your life to Celebrate with gratitude, and give your authentic self a deep, loving Embrace. Your true colors are beautiful. Bravo!

Refresher: **D**ance, **A**ffirmations, **N**otes, **C**elebration, **E**mbrace

DAY 8

NURTURE, NOURISHMENT, NEST

During the D.A.N.C.E., we can take time to Nurture and Nourish ourselves, our bodies, loved ones, pets, homes, gardens, etc. Has your body been trying to communicate a need? Have you been craving a particular food or activity? What is on both your 'to do' list AND your wish list? Could you give yourself a gift today? It could cost money like a massage at a spa, favorite take-out meal, or an inspiring art print. It could also be as simple as a compliment to yourself in the mirror, a phone call or letter to a friend, or a hot bath. To moms with babies, even time to take a shower is a gift!

Sometimes, I serenade myself with a love song, such as "You're in my heart and soul" by Rod Stewart or "All of Me" by John Legend. I change the words to say, "I give my all to you. I give my all to me. I give my all to us/life." referring to myself and the Divine within and around me. You could do something similar while taking a bath by candlelight. I suggest you keep the candle a safe distance from the water though. I once had a lit candle fall in the tub with me. The melted part quickly solidified into tiny bits and a big mess of wax confetti! It felt like an episode of a clumsy real house wife.

You could give yourself a foot massage after dancing today. I love using the lavender body butter from Thistle Farms for hands and feet before going to bed in the winter. Using their product feels like nourishing myself and others since their mission is to heal, employ, and empower women survivors of trafficking and addiction.

You could also nourish someone else today if you feel up for it. Is there something you've been thinking of doing for someone else and just haven't gotten around to yet? Is there a random act of kindness you'd enjoy doing soon? Do you have a pet that could use some mutual attention? My son often asks, "Have you pet your cat yet today?" I love how our cat, Koiya, brings sweet smiles to my boys! I wish we could purr like cats. It sounds delightful!

Could your home nest use a little attention or de-cluttering? My car could really use a cleaning more often. There are usually crumbs from who knows what in the backseat where the kids sit! My home is also very 'clutterful' since we homeschool, work from home, and spend the majority of our time in our home. The coffee table and couches are frequently covered in books, along with the dining table and chairs! Our home is very lived in. Though I don't love cleaning, it feels nourishing when our home feels more inviting. Even the simple act of putting some fresh flowers in a vase can be nurturing. I might take a small step like taking out the trash or cleaning the kitchen or a bigger step like cleaning out the fridge. My closet is another matter. There may be a few skeletons in there! I've started taking baby steps to get through it. It was about time to finally get rid of the shoes that no longer fit since my feet grew a size when I was pregnant, which was over a decade ago. Now, I'm singing "Footloose." Kick off your shoes today!

Seriously, though, I'm the queen of procrastination when it comes to household chores. I would love to have Samantha's abilities from the old television show *Bewitched* to clean the house with a wiggle of my nose! When my time comes, I don't think I'll regret choosing to paint, hike, dance, or daydream more often. So, please, do not let me bully or pressure you into cleaning house! Today is about nourishment. If, unlike me, you tend to keep a neat home, then nourishment may look the opposite for you. Take a break to nourish yourself today. Permission granted to procrastinate!

I had a flashback from the movie *Mr. Mom* while thinking about how to include men in the suggestions for today. Men can enjoy this stuff, too. Who doesn't love a great massage or delicious meal? My dad made decadent homemade hot chocolate for us when he was visiting and my boys love baking with grandmothers. One of them said if he has grandkids, they'll have a grandpa who bakes! We have an old set of bowls that was a wedding gift to my parents. We used them with my mom in the past. We remember a time my mom made a chocolate cake from scratch and accidentally dropped it bringing it to the table. It was a rare time I heard her curse! It was shortly before she died and I can only imagine the thoughts and emotions for her. We ate it anyway and that upside down chocolate cake made a sweet memory. Now, we say the secret ingredient is to mix in a 50 year old bowl full of love. Any bowl full of love will do!

What can you add to your D.A.N.C.E. today to nurture yourself? Maybe you could enjoy a nourishing cup of tea after dancing. You could use a fancy cup and add something fresh from outdoors to a charming vase or light a nice candle while having tea and taking your notes. I love a cool glass of water from our mountain well with fresh picked organic rose petals in summer. It smells heavenly when taking a sip! I'm thankful for whoever planted the roses by our porch before we moved here. I adore the vibrant, silky blooms. You could pick or buy some flowers for yourself today or plant something to nourish you in your yard or community. You could add a magic touch to your home or garden, such as wind chimes.

The urge to multi-task can be so strong I try to accomplish more stuff when driving or eating lunch on my porch, such as listening to a podcast or a book. Lately, I've been taking breaks to just sit with nature and myself instead, without even trying to meditate! It's nourishing. I invite you to 'sit a spell' as they say where I grew up.

Play host or hostess to your sacred self, be your own honored guest or enjoy some rest and relaxation during the D.A.N.C.E. today!

Refresher: **D**ance, **A**ffirmations, **N**otes, **C**elebration, **E**mbrace

DAY 9

COMMUNION, COLLECTIVE, COMFORT

The C in the D.A.N.C.E. can stand for Communion or Comfort. When seasons permit, I love Collecting a fresh rose petal, sage leaf, mint, rosemary, or something wild and edible from the yard, such as a clover, violet, or dandelion, for a sort of grateful communion with nature. My paternal grandparents were Catholic so I witnessed communion on the rare occasions that I went to church with them as a child. I suppose this is my version of a similar communion ritual with Mother Nature and Creation. Of course, please be sure you have the necessary knowledge to accurately identify what plant you have and that it is safe to eat before doing so!

I like to thank the plants for nourishing me with the vitality of the Earth from the roots, Fire from the Sun, Air and Water through the leaves. I love being able to take in all of the elements this way. I also think about any associations I'm familiar with or intuitively feel about the plant. For example, I might say a blessing like, "May I remember the wisdom from nature, my own beauty and magic, and to act with kindness towards all of creation" when eating rosemary, which is often associated with remembrance. I tend to thank the sage for wisdom and vitality or the mint for being refreshing and rejuvenating. The rose petals remind me to enjoy the sweetness.

Some days, I might incorporate communion by singing with the birds or hugging a tree instead. The C could also stand for Chilling out in a hammock in the trees. Sometimes, I'll dance in the mist since we often get misty mornings here in the ancient Appalachian Mountains. The mist feels like a gentle kiss from Mother Nature.

The word Collective makes me think about how we are all part of an amazing Circle of Life. It reminds me of ideas about sharing a collective consciousness. I think of lyrics from a song my husband wrote: "And maybe you and me are awake in the mind of God."

I'm reminded of a poem that has brought Comfort to people about *Footprints in the Sand.* My friend, Debbie, gave it to me years ago. It talks about God carrying us when times get tough or overwhelming or circumstances challenge us in life. At times like that, it may be harder to do the D.A.N.C.E. daily. I recognize that not everyone is comfortable with the term 'God' due to various reasons, stories, and beliefs. I enjoy the word 'Delight' for the Divine. I hope the time and energy spent doing the D.A.N.C.E. ritual may strengthen our spirits and be something to lean on. I hope tending to Delight when we're able to can help Divine Delight to comfort and carry us through other times. I think about people who seem to have a deep inner peace in spite of the drama in the world and drama in their personal lives. The D.A.N.C.E. ritual is a way to nurture peace and Delight within us. It has comforted me in some rough times when grieving, disappointed, hurting, confused, or afraid.

Collective also makes me think about being a collector and one of my favorite children's books, *Puddle Pail*, by Elisa Kleven. The main character collects reflections in a bucket of water. He later uses the water while making paintings inspired by the many beautiful scenes he saw and collected in the water. It makes me think of filling our buckets by collecting inspiration, beauty, wonder, love, and delight!

How can you add Communion with Creation to your Celebration today? I hope you Collect some beautiful visions and nourishment. May this ritual be a Comfort that can carry you through your days, including any drama, as you D.A.N.C.E. with Delight!

Refresher: **D**ance, **A**ffirmations, **N**otes, **C**elebration, **E**mbrace

DAY 10

ENJOY, ENTERTAIN, ENLIGHTEN

Enjoy, Entertain, and Enlighten are more of the many options for the letter E in the D.A.N.C.E! I love how the ritual often helps me to be more present and enjoy the moment. I love feeling lighter!

Laughter can be good medicine when it's not at someone else's expense or hurting someone else. I think entertaining ourselves and being silly can be, too. One day when I was at a botanical garden with my family, we saw statues of a boy chasing geese. I asked my boys if they wanted to go on a wild goose chase with me and take a picture. Neither of them chose to join me. I did it anyway! My son said, "I've always wondered how I ended up with a nutter for a mom." I haven't always allowed myself to be that silly and playful. When my boys were toddlers, they helped me to remember and taught me how to play again. Now, I love to play in so many ways!

I remember asking my husband if he was going to help me hide eggs for an Easter egg hunt for our boys. He said, "Aren't they too old for that now?" I replied, "No, I'm not too old for it so they aren't! Just because they're growing up doesn't mean they have to stop having fun." After the kids found all the eggs, I told them it was their turn to hide them. At first, it surprised them, but they quickly agreed. I love that my husband had fun finding them with me and racing to get to them before me! Afterwards, I asked the boys which was more fun, finding the eggs or hiding them. They said they enjoyed both! I intend to keep on playing as we get older.

I often greet a blank canvas as a playground for painting. We can greet life and our dance floor as a playground sometimes, too! I remember how free my kids used to be when they would dance as toddlers for pure fun. They had no reservations or concerns about what anyone else thought then. They went through a phase when they loved to dance to fast music. I don't even remember how we stumbled on the fast bluegrass song that was their favorite for a while. They filled the home with pure joy when they would dance back then. It was pretty entertaining, too! As teens, they've given up dancing. I hope that someday they will feel that free again.

As they gave it up, I did the opposite. Maybe it's a natural rhythm to go through phases and explore what we truly enjoy. Maybe it's a symptom of society. While writing in my notes about belonging to a community, I noticed an aspect of belonging that could feel like being owned! I'd rather be freely contributing to and cooperating in communities. I don't want to feel owned, the way things belong to people who own them, if I belong to a group. Ownership makes me wonder what's healthy and think of toddlers saying, "mine!" I remember a cat stuffed animal my boys loved. We named it 'Share' since we only had the one. When we found a similar dog later, they named it 'Sunny.' I don't think they had heard of Sonny and Cher!

Whatever your comfort level, I hope you can loosen up and lighten up today. That's what I mean by the word enlighten! Enjoy dancing freely and playfully. Do you know the chicken dance? What would it feel like to make funny faces while dancing? How can you add some silly fun and pure joy in your D.A.N.C.E. today?

Do you let yourself fully and freely lean in to joy? As I mentioned earlier regarding celebration, I noticed a while ago that when I felt joy, it was sometimes accompanied by guilt. If I started to feel 'too much' joy, my empathic body would start to feel guilty about it while so many people suffer. I'd feel bad for neglected and starving children or someone I knew that was going through chemotherapy. Compassion can be a beautiful thing that encourages us to lift one another up. Yet, I found that when I chose to shed the 'weight of the world' and allowed myself to fully experience shameless joy, I was actually more able to be generous and kind rather than fearful. I noticed feeling guilty about being joyful may have been associated with fear not just compassion, such as fear that I would go hungry or experience an illness. The guilt and fear were tainting my joy and weighing me down. From that state, I could get too overwhelmed and feel so helpless that I might give up on taking compassionate action. Falling into depression or hopelessness rarely helps anyone.

We are all worthy of joy! So, I'm allowing myself to feel shameless joy as often as I can. It makes me feel lighter and want to share the joy! The energy and enthusiasm feel much healthier and inspire me to have hope. The hope leads to action to be more kind, generous, encouraging, and to share sweetness, beauty, blessings, and fruit! When I feel good, I want others to feel good, too! I've learned that joy can have healthy ripple effects. What brings you joy?

Do you enjoy your own company? If so, that is truly wonderful! If not, what can you do to enjoy your own company more? Maybe you can find ways to entertain yourself. Entertain is a word that has more than one interesting definition to notice. It means to provide with amusement or enjoyment. It also means to give attention or consideration to. How can you give joy and attention to yourself? What makes you smile, laugh, or feel lighter? I adore giggles, hugs, raspberries, wild flowers, fireflies, my favorite windchimes, holding hands, purring cats, painting, feeling the Earth with bare feet, live music, seeing fish in the zen pond we made by our porch, sunsets, boat rides, walking by the water, stargazing, and of course, dancing! There are so many simple joys we can celebrate in our lives when we trust that feeling joy and feeling good are healthy for all of us.

I encourage you to lighten up, add some silly fun and lean in to shameless joy during your D.A.N.C.E. today. Dance with Delight!

Refresher: **D**ance, **A**ffirmations, **N**otes, **C**elebration, **E**mbrace

DAY 11

~⚜~

DRAW, DECIDE, DISCOVER

Draw, Decide and Discover are more possibilities for the D in the D.A.N.C.E! Have you ever used oracle cards, tarot, or any kind of inspiration cards before? If you have a deck you love, this can be a great way to start your daily D.A.N.C.E. by inviting inspiration and loving encouragement to influence your affirmations and notes.

I think of inspiration, oracle, and tarot cards as tools, like a radio antenna, that can help us to have less static and tune in to our own wisdom more clearly using the imagery and ideas as prompts. First, I like to pause and take a nice deep breath. I usually invite beautiful blessings and loving guidance before selecting a card. If something has been on my mind, I may focus on that. You can shuffle the deck and choose a card or two blindly from anywhere in the deck or you can look through the cards with the word/art sides facing you to intuitively choose a card you see that sings to you today.

I love that this idea happened to fall on day 11, which is a number often associated with angel messengers. Oracle cards can also be like messengers. Last year, I kept drawing two cards more often than any others: Dance and Ritual! I kept doing both. Those cards were like cheerleaders encouraging me even though I didn't know why at the time. Many moons later, this book has been written! I also decided to keep two cards from decks I created myself by me while writing the book: Confidence and Liberation. I let them cheer me on to remind me to trust myself and speak freely.

On days I choose a card before dancing, I might take the card into consideration while saying affirmations or use the card as a journal or prayer prompt when taking notes. I've come to love collecting and using oracle card decks for inspiration, a tool for tuning in to my own inner wisdom, for the energy and for the beautiful art. I choose decks created by others carefully. I only decide to use cards that I love. I've also created my own decks. If you don't have any, you could use a pen or pencil to draw a card of your own today and choose a message or idea that inspires you. It can be as simple as a favorite word, symbol, or a doodle in your notebook! You decide.

While I was writing this book, all sorts of doubts started popping up as I thought about what type of book it was. I thought my first book would be about mixed media art rather than what may be called 'self help.' I started thinking, "who am I to talk about that or appear as if I have answers when I'm constantly asking questions, changing my mind, and trying different things?!"

I get triggered by words. I've noticed how the words we decide to use can have a big impact on how we feel. I was blessed with a new perspective to re-interpret the words 'self help.' I saw that I've been writing the story of my own self help, as in how I've been helping myself to dance with delight, almost like a memoir of sorts. I also revised the words in my head to see it being more about wonder, exploration, discovery, delight, vitality, celebration, creativity, and rejuvenation. I felt better about it. I'm drawn to these subjects. I'm full of wonder. I love to explore life, including getting to know myself better and being more aware and creative with my choices.

One of the reasons I love the creative process and making intuitive art is because I've discovered so much healing medicine and many magical messages that way. I've found intuitive writing can also be full of discoveries! I make discoveries while interpreting inspiration and oracle cards for myself as well. Even thinking about our doubts can lead to discoveries and decisions. I remember two different events with small circles of women when I declared and decided to release so much self doubt. I've learned to trust myself more deeply since making that decision.

Now, I see this book is about life choices and exploration through experimentation with the various ideas and activities. You can see if anything appeals to you and what aspects you decide to include in your daily D.A.N.C.E. if you decide to go forward with the ritual on your own. It's also about self discovery as you explore the inquiries and tune in to your own heart songs and life. In spite of my doubts and even though I have other books in progress, it turns out that the first one to flow fully forth is about the art of living and loving, including the creative process, decisions, and discovery!

The song, "How do you talk to an Angel?" came into my head. It makes me think about discovery and how we talk to the Divine within and around us. I feel like I communicate with muses, angel messengers, and divine mystery through reading, writing, painting, dancing, music, prayer, and exploring the natural world. If I'm tired of feeling depleted or desperate, I invite Delight to join me instead!

Today, I encourage you to dive in to your own discoveries during your D.A.N.C.E. time. You could draw an oracle card. You could ask yourself what you may be doubting or feeling more drawn to at this point in your life journey. You could make a decision.

You can explore your physical body during the movement of your D.A.N.C.E. to see if there is anything you may discover that way. I have discovered that I love the feel of a soft sage leaf or rose petal on my skin and lips, like a gentle caress from Mother Nature. You can allow your discoveries or decisions to guide your Affirmations and your Notes, Celebrate, and give yourself a loving Embrace.

You can Decide to Dance with Delight!

Refresher: **D**ance, **A**ffirmations, **N**otes, **C**elebration, **E**mbrace

If the suggestions on any day don't interest you, simply skip that!

DAY 12

ASK, ALLOW, ACCEPT, APPRECIATE

May we Allow, Accept and Appreciate the blessings in our lives with receptive open hands, heads, and hearts for the letter A in the D.A.N.C.E. today. Acceptance is a big topic! Many of us long to feel accepted. We might long to accept more wealth or have more well being. We may find it challenging to accept some people or circumstances. Today, you can use this as a journal prompt to take notes about what the word/idea of Acceptance brings up for you.

If you are longing to feel more accepted, how can you accept your self more fully? You might refer back to ideas from previous days about embracing and loving your body or speaking to yourself kindly in the mirror through affirmations. I love a line in the book, *A Wrinkle in Time* by Madeleine L'Engle, when one character offers the main character her faults as a gift. Those 'faults' end up serving her well. I've been thinking about how I can do the same thing and accept any apparent faults as gifts. For example, I tend to be very sensitive. I've decided that using my senses to enjoy the sweet soft pleasures in life is a sensational gift. I can also see being stubborn, a trait that I share with my boys, as persistence. May we use it wisely!

I'm learning to tap in to my sensitivity in healthier ways after years of letting the need for external approval and acceptance stifle me. I wanted to be accepted by others so much growing up that I didn't think to ask myself what I wanted to allow or accept. I liked school and had nice teachers who taught what was deemed appropriate. I went with the program. I let others determine what I should learn so that I'd be successful and how I should look, dress, or act to be considered pretty and be popular. It led to spots on a cheerleading squad, dance team, top of the class, and academic scholarships for bachelors and masters degrees. It didn't lead to wisdom, kindness, curiosity, true confidence, delight, self-love, respect, or acceptance. Some may think I'm wasting my potential not using the degrees. I wonder if it's wasted now or then. I wonder about the economic idea of earning a living rather than accepting life as a gift we share.

I'm taking responsibility for my own choices now. I'm listening to my heart and accepting myself. I still find it challenging sometimes, especially while I'm raising children. I catch myself wondering what others might think, not just about me, but about my children also! I don't want to pass my own insecurities on to them. I wonder if I've done the right thing attempting to raise them to accept and trust themselves rather than to be popular or fit in. Most of the time, I think so. I'm glad that my children seem to feel comfortable being themselves. My husband and I were wondering why a few famous people committed suicide recently when our son overhead us from another room and remarked, "those people don't give themselves enough credit." While there's more to it than that, I'm glad he has such an awareness of self worth that I didn't have when I was 13!

I remember a song that touched my heart the first time I heard it, and my husband shared the same song with me soon after. It was "My Wish" by Rascal Flatts. It was new and we were new parents. It was a sweet moment of our hopes colliding. It has surprised me to learn how many people I have known, who seemed to have it all together or be the life of the party, who were hiding depression or anxiety behind cocktails or convincing smiles. It's my wish for all of us to make the choices that mean the most to us, to feel loved as we are, and still be able to pay the bills and enjoy full, rich lives!

I've noticed that when I take myself less seriously and allow myself to loosen up and 'just be me' rather than looking to anyone else for approval and acceptance, it feels liberating! I've jokingly thought of going to 'be me' school instead of 'busy-ness' school! I also cheer myself on now with the phrase "be you to full" to encourage and allow a more genuine and loving kind of beautiful acceptance. I still wish to feel accepted in healthy community also. I've imagined and defined what 'healthy' community actually means to me. I've said, "I welcome connections with kindred spirits. I am a natural part of the circle of life. I belong. It is okay to be seen as I am. I enjoy casual, loving, and intimate relationships with mutual appreciation. I am worthy of love and life and joy! While I receive input from others, I love, trust, value, allow, appreciate, and accept myself."

I love how the word 'appreciate' means both to be thankful about something and also to grow or expand! If you are longing to accept more wealth or well being, you can notice more of the blessings and abundance that you already have in your life right here and now. Appreciate your blessings to watch the blessings appreciate and expand. Shifting our focus from longing to what we are and have in this moment creates a different feeling. For me, longing doesn't feel great. Appreciation and celebration feel much better! One day, I found myself saying, "take my longing and turn it into love." You can probably fill at least one whole page in your notes about things you appreciate and feel fortunate to have, experience, or love in your life now, including some we often take for granted.

For example, "I'm grateful for clean water and hot showers (can you tell we had a plumbing problem?). I love healthy and delicious options from near and far at a local grocery store. I gladly accept the wealth and bounty life offers me. I'm glad someone invented eye glasses and electricity. I love cozy blankets. I love the taste of ripe strawberries and shucking corn with family in "summertime" and singing with Will Smith. I love crisp autumn air and colorful leaves. I love feeling sunshine on my face and wind in my hair. I'm blessed here now." We can also bring past and future ideas into the present moment in healthier ways, using a voice of love that makes us smile, rather than dwelling too much on lack or longing. For example, "I love the memories of the sparkles in my mom's eyes and the sweet way she smiled when playing with her grandkids." and "I love having many opportunities to share joy, magic, and beauty with others through books, art, and presentations. I'm glad that the internet enables me to share so easily. I love exploring this planet and meeting interesting people. I love feeling good!"

I revise the song "Fortunate Son" to say I am a fortunate one! Try this yourself. Keep going until you feel deeply, truly blessed in the present moment. As mentioned earlier, when focusing on authentic affirmations, choose words or visions that feel true to ALL of you, your whole being, so both your heart and head are in harmony!

If you still feel longing, notice whether you are addressing fears or appreciating loves. Consider what acceptance and wealth mean to you. Sometimes, we've accepted definitions and ideals from others or the media that may not be true for us. I feel rich whether my appearance fits anyone else's definition of rich or not. I think of a rich life as broader than having expensive stuff, though money is a tool I gladly accept and use to enjoy a rich life. Is there something you need permission to do, be, or feel? Can you give yourself that permission? Do you trust yourself enough to allow or accept whatever wonderful wildest dreams you can imagine? Remember the 'Oh Yeah' trick from day 2! Visualize, accept, and feel appreciation for the pure potential and possibilities in each magic moment.

Are you open to divine blessings, synchronicity, and guidance? Do you ask for, allow, and accept it? I've even asked divine guidance to clearly show me the way as if hitting me over the head with it so that I cannot miss it! At times, I've felt frustrated when no obvious "signs" like Tesla sings about seem to help guide my way. So, I feel forced, or I mean guided, to look within and trust myself then. Still, I've been amazed how much I experience sweet synchronicity since becoming more open to it. I've been given spots in several online art courses. I've also received a scholarship for a local art course. I made efforts to reciprocate, such as purchasing other courses from the artists who's give-aways I've accepted and volunteering at the local folk school where I received a scholarship. I pay it forward by giving away spots in courses I host and free gifts. My librarians save donated books they think I'll enjoy for me. They gave one to me recently, and I gave them a donation. The book was about letting the Divine take the lead! It was waiting there for me after I'd asked for guidance. I think about asking and the power of invitation. I feel a subtle shift in energy or intention from demanding, chasing, or begging! I ask and invite the Divine to dance with me, bless me with healthy connections, and guide my path with joy.

I've experimented with leaving room for the magic, miracles, and mystery to bless me while still speaking clearly about my hopes and dreams. I've described a dream team I'd love to work, collaborate, and dance with. I've consider the idea of "this or something better" to allow space for wholiness to bless me "beyond what I can ask or imagine" in healthy ways for me and "all my relations." I have used my Sacred Breath to blow dandelion seeds while saying, "I wish for guidance and grace to bless my family in whatever ways are best for us to accept and enjoy freedom, fulfillment, and feeling fabulous!"

Today, let's focus on what we allow, accept, and appreciate. You can ask for, invite, and accept wellness, which can include wealth, using affirmations, such as, "I am ready, willing, able, and open to give and receive with ease. I invite, allow, appreciate and accept healthy options and abundance in my life with grace, gratitude, joy, and wisdom. My life is enriching! I am Delightfull." Oh Yeah!

Allow yourself to enjoy and celebrate the beautiful blessings within you and around you. Accept that you are worthy just the way you are. You have all that you need within you to thrive true. You are a magnificent part of the circle of life! Accept your whole sacred self.

You are beautiful. Be you to full. Let your heart sing. Appreciate, Allow, and Accept Delight during the D.A.N.C.E!

Refresher: **D**ance, **A**ffirmations, **N**otes, **C**elebration, **E**mbrace

DAY 13

NATURAL NATURE

Another option for the N in D.A.N.C.E. is nature or natural. Since I have twins, the topic of nurture versus nature has come up often. I've witnessed plenty of the 'nature' aspect to their personalities in addition to the role of nurturing. How do you feel about your own true Nature? I've been thinking about my own original nature and original innocence lately.

I invite you to explore your true nature with these prompts today:

❖ Who would you be if you were born into a different time or place? What time and place would you live in if you could choose? These questions can hold clues about how we are influenced by cultures, situations, and surroundings.

❖ Do you know the song lyrics, "You make me feel like a natural woman" by Carole King? What makes you feel like your natural self? Does any way of being or activity seem to come naturally to you? Where do you feel at home?

❖ Are there any other animals you cross paths with often or feel drawn to that have qualities you admire or embody? You can type "Spirit Animal questionnaire" into an online search engine to fill one out if that interests you.

❖ What if nature, including human nature, is pure potential?

❖ What if eternal Wholiness and Liveliness is wild and free?

❖ If you were in a plentiful garden paradise, would you enjoy sharing any delicious, nourishing fruit?

❖ What does paradise mean to you? What if no one was ever cast out? What if heaven includes our place on earth?

Now, I'm singing "Almost Paradise" or "Para-Para-Paradise." You could consider the above questions while dancing or taking notes today. Exploring those questions has helped me to revise some old ideas I had picked up about people and myself. It's helped me to be more confident and trust myself. Learning to trust myself has made a difference in what I'm able to imagine, accept, share, and enjoy.

We could also think of the aspect of the word nature that refers to the natural world and get outside today! My dad's loving partner, Jane, refers to nature as her cathedral. Though I didn't have such a great way to say it before, I have felt similarly most of my life. I'm thankful that my parents shared such a deep love and reverence for nature as they nurtured me, from a farm in the mountains to what they considered a paradise in the islands. Still, I admit that I don't love mosquitoes as much as mosquitoes love me!

Is there somewhere you could D.A.N.C.E. in the woods, amongst wild flowers, beneath a starry sky, or at the water's edge today? You could even take a nap or sleep outside tonight as Dave Matthews suggests in the song, "One Sweet World." Getting out of a house, office, or other manmade building might help us to tune in to our original, wild, divine, pure energy and true nature.

How do you feel about being 'au naturel?' The translation of the French phrase is 'in the natural.' When I looked it up online, one of the meanings was 'with no elaborate treatment or preparation.' Another was 'pristine.' I love the idea of being pristine, without any elaborate preparation, just the way we are 'in the natural.' We are pristine, as in original and pure, at the core of our true nature.

I've been visualizing my sacred self like a clear prism. I was gifted with this vision when I was dancing in my pajamas. My shirt had a sparkling snowflake on it that was reflecting the sunshine in the living room windows. I've always loved prisms and rainbows. My parents had a prism hanging by the front door of our home. My mom gave us one when my husband and I had our first home. It hangs in my art studio now. The front door of our home has cut glass that scatters rainbows on the floor and walls as the sun goes down each evening. The door was already here and the rainbows were a lovely unexpected gift when we moved in. What if our original nature is like a pure and clear prism for the presents and presence of Divine Delight to shine through? Maybe as we reconnect with our Source, clear away any stains and illusions, and let Delight shine through us, we can create rainbows in a seemingly stormy world. I think of the song "Heal this Land" by Tina Malia.

While thinking about prisms, I thought of both inexpensive glass and more pricey diamonds. I no longer place the kind of value on diamonds that jewelry stores do. To me, the value of a diamond ring isn't the financial price. The deeper value is from and in the love that it symbolizes. A diamond isn't this girl's best friend. My husband is. I've never really noticed a difference between diamonds and cubic zirconia. Even glass made from sand can cast rainbows like more expensive diamonds. Fragile spider webs, water drops, and snowflakes also sparkle with rainbows as light shines on them.

I love how snowflakes are all the same kind of thing and also each unique. According to some scientific ideas, diamonds, glass, sand, water, and each of us are all made up of the same stuff, stardust. I didn't understand much in physics class, but I like the poetic sound of stardust and the idea that we all have the same core worth. Let your inner light shine to create brilliant rainbows all around you!

D.A.N.C.E. with pure, pristine Delight in Nature's Cathedral today.

Refresher: **D**ance, **A**ffirmations, **N**otes, **C**elebration, **E**mbrace

DAY 14

⁓⟪❧⟫⁓

CREATE & CO-CREATE

Letting the C in D.A.N.C.E. stand for Create immediately brings two things to mind for me. As an artist and painter, I think of creating with our hands and raw materials, such as art supplies, cooking ingredients, or building supplies. I also think about co-creating ourselves and our lives! A great way to combine the ideas is to create a gratitude collage, vision board, or an art journal page.

I invite you to use and enjoy your creative gift today. Listen to and trust your instincts, visions, inspiration, voice, heart and soul. No matter what some fine art critics or art teachers may say, we can all be artists! I often greet the blank surface as both a playground and a temple, a place to meet with mystery, explore the wonders and my own wilderness, play with possibility, sing, pray, cry, celebrate and co-create with the life force that flows through all!

I'm so thankful to have what I call my M.F.A., as in the Magic and Medicine Found in Art! That's what I've found while exploring the creative process through intuitive and inquisitive mixed media art. Making art has been such a healing, playful, spiritual joy for me. I'm grateful that having kids gave me an excuse to pick up crayons and play with paint again after leaving a corporate career. I hope you still allow yourself to have art supplies in your life. If, like me, you thought you had to 'put away childish things' and have no art supplies, I invite, encourage, and give you permission to play with paint, glue, and collage.

Creating intuitive art is another way to get in touch with your own authentic voice and original nature. It is a way to make room for and meet with the Divine within and around us. Today, I invite you to visualize while dancing or create a page in your book of notes about your visions. You could also add collage to your journal if you have the time, energy, and desire. You could even turn your journal for notes into an art journal if you like.

I've made vision boards since before I had ever heard the term 'vision board.' As a teen, I made collages with magazines for the covers of my binders and notebooks. You could do that with the cover for your notes book! I've also done collages with corkboards since I was a teenager. Now, I use collage and journaling in mixed media paintings as well. I approach the idea of vision boards a bit differently than focusing on specific goals or manifestation.

If you would like to make a collage for your co-creative envisioning today, find an old magazine or book that you are willing to tear or cut up. While browsing the magazine or book, collect any words and imagery that whisper, sing, or shout out to you. Trust your instincts and what inspires you. You might be surprised by what you are drawn to, hear, and discover. I think of this as a way to let our inner wisdom, Sacred Spirit, and Divine Mystery speak to us.

You could also use your own photographs, art, or mementos. You could focus on how you love to feel rather than on physical things. You could also look at your vision board as an offering to life and a way to celebrate what you are thankful for right now. I often think of this as a kind of prayer, whether hopeful, grateful, or both. I've also thought of it as spelling out prayers or casting magic spells. I'm a fan of the *Harry Potter* books by J.K. Rowling along with more down to earth magic books, wizards, and wise women. I sometimes think of vision boards as dream catchers and dream weaving. I also try to remember "sometimes I thank God for unanswered prayers" like Garth Brooks. That song rang true to me when I first heard it in junior high school and had some crazy crushes.

Notice how you feel through the process. If fears come up, what can relieve them? How can you lean in to love and delight now?

Once you have a collection of collage material, you can arrange it and adhere it to your note book cover, a page inside your notebook or a different surface in any way you like. I prefer gel medium or Mod Podge adhesive for mixed media art, but I used whatever I had as a teen. Glue, glue sticks, or tape will work. After arranging the collage, you can add any affirmations, favorite quotes, lyrics, or words that feel inspiring or enriching in your own handwriting with pen or marker. Many of the paintings I included in my inspiration card decks were created this way. I paired them with words, ideas, and feelings that seem like blessings to me, such as Vitality.

If you don't have the time or desire to use art supplies today, you could mentally visualize the life you are co-creating by using your amazing imagination, affirmations, and celebration while dancing. You could browse a magazine or online (artistic social media pages or pinterest with a timer so you don't get lost) to see what visually makes your heart sing without actually using it for collage. It's still a way to listen to your instincts and explore what inspires you right now. You could invite loving guidance and serendipity. Then, you can mentally reference the imagery and make it your own using your imagination and visualization.

I love the idea of revising messages we find from media to be in tune with our own core values and create our own visions instead. I've also done this for visions of healthy co-ops and communities.

D.A.N.C.E. with Creation and your inner Magical Muse today.

Let Your Heart Sing!

Refresher: **D**ance, **A**ffirmations, **N**otes, **C**elebration, **E**mbrace

If the suggestions on any given day don't interest you, simply skip that and do the basic steps as suggested on the first day instead.

DAY 15

EXHALE, EAT, EXPRESS

The E in D.A.N.C.E. can remind us to eat and exhale or express, forming a natural rhythm of in and out. This step relates to the earlier idea about communion to me as well. I often think of being connected to and sharing my breath with others, whether people, animals, plants or Mother Earth, while enjoying deep breaths.

Take a moment to notice your breathing. Breathe in deeply and exhale fully to let all of the air out. When exhaling, we can focus our attention and intention on anything we might need or want to release and let go of, including tension in the body! If you're able to stand on the Earth with bare feet, you can exhale and give anything to the Earth that needs transforming into richer, healthy soil. You could imagine blowing dandelion seeds as you exhale to give your wishes to Life to let them go and grow where and how they will thrive. You could also exhale as if you were blowing bubbles. The motion with the mouth helps to focus on the act of exhaling. I like the idea of blowing out anything we'd like to release in the bubbles, such as any pain, stories, doubts, regrets, or illusions we're ready to change or let go of. You can imagine yourself popping the bubbles!

Each exhale is followed by an inhale, as is the natural rhythm of our bodies and life as we know it, similar to the ocean tides going out and back in again. Though we don't need to 'inhale' food the same way we inhale air, we do benefit from healthy appetites, both physically and symbolically. I didn't have a healthy relationship with my appetite and ambition for much of my life. I learned it wasn't appealing or attractive for women to have big appetites. I've known many women, including myself, who have struggled with eating disorders so I know I'm not the only one who has experienced this. While it impacted my dietary choices, it affected much more in my life that I wasn't aware of until later. I see that the hesitance and discomfort I've felt relating to achievement and ambition were also influenced by external views about greed, gluttony, sin, hunger and desire. I had deep core wounds about worthiness that I've been healing layer by layer. Men may also face an aspect of this, whether pressure to have bigger or smaller appetites/ambition or associate those with core worth. I invite you to consider your own beliefs about appetite, ambition, and worth today. The ideas about our true nature and potential from day 13 have helped me with this.

We can tune in to any feelings we may need to let flow through and let out today as well. All of our feelings are part of life. It is natural to feel sad, frustrated, hungry or empty as well as full, fabulous, or free. Lean in to whatever you are feeling right now to feel through it. If you are feeling anything that you are tempted to suppress or avoid, Exhale and Express it so you don't get stuck in that muck!

As I was writing this, we discovered that our neighbor's house was broken into during an evening walk. The thieves had cut our fence to drive through the field and access the neighbor's house. At first, I felt sick to my stomach with nerves, anxiety, and fear. Then, I felt disappointed and angry. I didn't want to let anyone steal my happy! I went outside onto the back porch in the dark, put on the happy song by Pharrell Williams, declared that 'Happiness is my truth,' and danced with the full moon. It helped. Yet, I still felt bad vibes and exhausted later that night when discussing it with my husband. Eventually, I prayed for healing, well being, and returning to love for whoever did it. That helped me start returning to love.

The next morning, I prayed again during my D.A.N.C.E. ritual. I remembered the lines from *Desiderata* by Max Ehrmann, which I'm so grateful my parents shared with me as I was growing up. The last lines have been a real gift to me when facing times like that. They remind me that, in spite of sham and broken dreams, there is still beauty in the world. That thought made me start singing to the tune from the *Addam's Family* television show to describe the world saying, "It's creepy and it's kooky. It's really kinda spooky." And yet, as Macy Gray sings, "There is beauty in the world!" Combining the songs to make a fun medley and choosing my inner soundtrack with awareness is a coping mechanism for me. It's a way to shift my energy and reclaim my own power to dance with delight. I felt lighter and richer, full of life and love. I felt better! I let the truth of my feelings out and danced with them until I started to feel "Good Vibrations" as the Beach Boys sing about! It's all part of the dance.

When I was heavy with grief after my mom died, I listened to sad songs and melancholy music. As Elton John says, "sad songs say so much." I let those feelings flow to move through the deepest grief. I didn't let myself keep listening to the sad stuff to prolong it though! I needed to move on to truly enjoy more uplifting music and moments. You can throw any feelings into the motions of the daily dance and let the feelings move you and move through you.

I can use my head to help my feelings flow in smarter ways. I don't want to yell, throw my emotions onto others, or harm anyone else. I'm less likely to "explode," as my son described it, if I don't let an emotional fire build and heat up inside like a volcano. I'm less likely to drown in tears if I let them flow rather than blocking them until they cause a flood. I prefer to let any mucky feelings out in healthy ways, like writing and dancing, so I can feel delightful more often!

I notice common letters in the words 'emotions' and the 'motions' of dance movement. It seems like our emotions are meant to be in constant motion, fluid, and flowing forth. The origin of the word emotion is related to moving and moving out! 'Express' can also mean to get the juice out of something! Express your feelings. Let your emotions move on through and flow out during your dance.

Keeping the natural rhythm of in and out, breathe in again. What have you been feeding yourself, both your body and your head, heart, and soul? There is junk food for the soul as well as the body. I've learned that I am quite sensitive to the visual and mental input I expose myself to. This is a reminder I need myself. I start to feel it when I forget or witness extra drama or satire. The days of our lives seem enough like a soap opera already for me. I rarely watch sports or news shows anymore for that reason. We cancelled cable before we moved way out 'in the sticks' where it's not an option.

We still enjoy high speed internet for work, curiosity, connections, expression, and entertainment. I prefer having my 'feed' and inbox be full of uplifting stories, poetic words, natural wonder, beautiful places, inspiring art, and kindred spirits. I'm being more intentional with the time I spend online, how, and who I spend it with. I adore many online friends from all around the world. Yet, I had enough popularity games in high school. So, I'm experimenting with the idea of 'less is more' to find a better balance. Too often, I'd pick up my phone, which I rarely use for calls, get distracted and forget why I picked it up! Less social media means more free time, more room for intuition and creativity, and I'm more present with family.

Notice how you feel when you read, watch, or listen to something. What inspires you? Do you have a healthy balance between media input and creative output? Breathe in and breathe out. It baffles me that I didn't value my own creativity for too long. I've always loved other artists, painters, poets, and writers. I've found what they offer valuable and worth purchasing. Yet, it took me years to finally see that my own creations are valuable in the same way. So are yours!

Today, I hope you can Enjoy some sweet soul food and Eat some nourishing food for your body. Take in a deep breath. Then, let out a big, full Exhale or a lion's roar if you feel the desire. Let it all out in your D.A.N.C.E. today. Express Yourself! Get to the Juicy stuff!

Refresher: **D**ance, **A**ffirmations, **N**otes, **C**elebration, **E**mbrace

DAY 16

DANCE IN THE DARKNESS,
DANCE WITH YOUR SHADOW

Today, we acknowledge Darkness with the letter D in D.A.N.C.E. I find it interesting that many stories associate darkness with the opposite of good, such as the 'Dark Side' of 'The Force' from the *Star Wars* movies. I was considering this recently when it happened to be a half moon in appearance (1st or 3rd quarter in a moon cycle). When I see a half moon, it tends to evoke a feeling of balance and equilibrium to me. The same is true with a yin and yang symbol.

We have a permaculture garden and have planted many fruit and nut trees, in addition to herb gardens and seasonal gardens. While thinking about light and darkness, I thought of the fruit trees. I see dark soil as rich and healthy! The trees use both the dark soil and the sunlight to produce sweet, tart, nourishing, delicious fruit! I've written affirmations and celebrated blessings on notes that I've actually planted in the Earth while planting seeds in the garden. It's a ritual I've done a few times on or soon after a dark new moon as a sliver of light increases. Is there anything you'd like to plant in the rich, fertile darkness to let it grow forth into light and bear fruit?

Darkness also makes me think of dark wombs that miraculously grow life. I was born on February 2nd. My birthday falls on what's known as Groundhog Day here in the United States. I was often teased on my birthday about whether or not I had seen my shadow like the groundhog. Maybe that made me more interested in and intimate with my shadow. I've enjoyed playing with my shadow since I was a young child, before I had ever heard of Carl Jung or psychological ideas about a shadow side of personality. Since then, I've explored that kind of intellectual idea and my own 'shadows' as well. Most of my life, I didn't know that my birthday also usually falls on the traditional Celtic holiday called Imbolc, which relates to the first signs of spring. It's interesting to me that Imbolc is usually associated with light or the return of the light and candles are lit. Candlemas falls on the same day. My birthday has shadow and light associated with it, as do we all in both physical and symbolic ways.

I wonder if seasons affect our relationships with dark and light. In winter, the warmth of sunshine can be such a blessing. In summer, the dark of the shade can be such a relief from the heat! Have you given much thought to ideas about light and dark? Have you been afraid of the dark? I have! Are you comfortable with the unknown?

I've also wondered about what happens when the 'light' goes out of our physical body. Death isn't something a lot of people in the United States are very comfortable talking about or thinking much about. Some cultures seem to handle it better than others. Some devote specific times to acknowledge this, such as the Day of the Dead in Mexico, or areas and activities in the home, such as shrines on shelves for ancestors in Japan. If you've experienced the death of a close loved one like I have, you've probably given it a bit of thought and maybe a river full of tears to let the grief flow.

Regardless of what physically or spiritually happens after death, I've experienced that the light and love continue to live on in the hearts and memories of loved ones like me. My mom was and still is one of my best friends. I don't think that I've ever communicated with spirits the same way a medium might. Yet, I still talk to my mom, especially while star gazing from my porch, going for a walk around our home, or walking in the woods. I still dance with her often while I'm painting or taking a dance break in my creative space.

Sometimes, the tears flow since I miss her and love her so much, especially when there is something big I want to share with her. Other times, I feel full of light and joy as I dance in her presence.

My friend, Amy, shared the song, "Dance in the Graveyards" by Delta Rae, with me after her mom died. The song was pretty new at the time. It felt like a message from her beloved momma. My mom chose to have her ashes buried in gardens and with a sugar maple tree in the wild rather than in a graveyard. Still, I promptly bought the song and started playing it loudly while driving in the car, singing and dancing along with my mom's joyful loving legacy. It was therapeutic! I think it was also a good example for my boys to see me dancing in joy after witnessing me shed so many tears.

I remember shortly before my mom died when we were on the way to one of my grandparent's funerals together. I think my boys were 4 years old. As we drove by a cemetery, one of my kids wondered, "So, heaven's underground?" That question sparked an interesting conversation! We discussed various ideas about heaven that are not underground. Still, it is the dark ground from which the seeds and roots of nourishment and life we experience on Earth grow. Now, I often tend to refer to heaven as the heavenly mystic or the mystic beyond. My mom loved Van Morrison. I chose the song "Into the Mystic" for the last song of the soundtrack for her life celebration memorial video. I love that my boys, who were only 5 when she died, now call all the songs from that video 'Grammie's songs.'

I remember the last morning with my mom before she died. She was no longer able to communicate verbally. I had been stubbornly holding on to her. I felt that I finally had to let her go. It felt selfish to keep denying it. I took the ring off her finger that she had tried to give to me the week before. I had told her that I wasn't ready yet then. This time, I told her I knew I had to let go and I wanted her to be free. She took her last breath soon after. In shock, I told my 5 year old boys, who'd been in a different room in the house, it was Grammie's birthday in heaven. We went out for chocolate cake.

Later, I stumbled upon a touching poem about the life cycles of a dragonfly symbolizing death as mysterious transformation. I read it at her memorial. It soothed my soul. I sign my art with my initials, J.O., in a cursive way that resembles a dragonfly to me in memory of her loving legacy. I can hear Axl Rose singing Paul McCartney's lyrics to, "Live and Let Die." I'll sing my own version, "Sometimes, you give in and cry... Live and let live... Live and let fly."

I'm a very visual person and learner. Did you ever play the game Blind Man's Bluff as a kid? We used to like playing it in the dark at a friend's farmhouse or in the basement when I was in elementary school. I remember trying to find my way around in the dark and blindfolded. I also remember trying to get 'in the map' like Joey from the *Friends* TV show to get a better visual, even in broad daylight, to find the way when I was in Europe with my friend, Kane. We can't always see in the dark or see the path we are on in life or what the next steps are. The silly song from the cartoon *Dora the Explorer* that my kids used to watch comes to mind. "I'm the map, I'm the map..." I wonder if we may be both the explorer and the map. I think of using our intuition, inner guidance, and tuning in to a kind of inner map or compass to find our way in the dark.

After watching the *Star Wars VIII* movie, I recall a scene when one of the characters is sitting with eyes closed to feel 'The Force.' I sometimes enjoy closing my eyes to tune into my other senses more, preferably without the hum of electronics. We can feel the energy and life within and around us without using our eyes to see, create, or differentiate amongst forms. Think about how much time we'd spend in darkness if it weren't for electricity! I don't take it for granted, but I wonder how we'd spend that time differently, such as dancing, dreaming, storytelling, wondering, and resting.

You could close your eyes and be still for a while or try exploring in a safe place with your eyes closed today. "Hello, darkness, my old friend..." I'm singing with Simon & Garfunkel, some of my first sing along friends as a toddler according to my Mom. It brings back a fun memory when my brother, Cy, called them "Garfield and Funkel" on a road trip when we were young.

Thinking of darkness also reminds me of dark stones that are said to have healing properties. My son has a piece of obsidian he chose at a rock shop a few years ago. He told me it is supposed to help with anger and frustration. I've since learned many black stones, such as onyx, can help detoxify, absorb, and clear negative energy.

We had a black cat show up for a while that seemed to be adopting us. I started calling it Sid, for Obsidian, or Onyx, or Oreo because it had a tiny patch of white on the tummy. I've found that petting a purring black cat (or any nice pet) can help to dissolve negativity and be soothing as well. I've heard that black cats are less likely to find a home due to superstitions where I live. I think loving one can help us let go of that stuff, too. I'm singing along with Stevie Wonder saying, "superstition ain't the way."

I invite you to get a bit more comfortable, or at least intimate, with darkness, your shadow, and the mystic unknown today. If the time of day and weather permit, you can go outside and dance with your own shadow. I love to do that in the early morning or late evening when the shadows are so long! I've thought of my ego as a sort of guardian shadow. You could dance with your guardian.

You could dance with your eyes closed or join Bruce Springsteen "Dancing in the Dark!" You could dance in the graveyards or into the mystic if there is someone that you'd love to dance with some more. You could think of dancing with a guardian angel(s).

D.A.N.C.E. with both the Darkness and Delight today.

Refresher: **D**ance, **A**ffirmations, **N**otes, **C**elebration, **E**mbrace

If the suggestions on any given day don't interest you, simply skip that and do the basic steps as suggested on the first day instead.

DAY 17

AWARE, ATTENTION, ALTAR, ANCESTRY

To me, part of the value of ritual is taking time to slow down as we become more Aware of our own thoughts and actions to choose what we are giving Attention to. Sometimes, we can get so caught up in all of the responsibilities and tasks that make up our days that we seem to go on autopilot. When I was very sleep deprived from having two babies waking up during the night to be fed (and having alarms go off in the middle of the night since they both came home from the hospital with oxygen support and two monitors each), it's a good thing I was able to function on autopilot somehow! I didn't know what a blessing cordless babies were before. There are times when circumstances demand our attention, such as with newborn babies or illness. Yet, when able, it's worthwhile to use awareness to notice and choose what we give attention to as much as we can.

In any given moment, our thoughts might run away to dwell on past events and regrets or run ahead to worry about future bills, health, etc. Yet, in order to learn from the past and plan for the future, it helps to be aware of the thoughts and choose which ones we give attention to now. Both our attention and our intentions are powerful. When we give attention to our daily choices, energy, and actions, we also support our broader, bigger intentions. What we give our attention to now also impacts how present we are in each marvelous moment. Choosing affirmations, celebrating, and taking notes during the D.A.N.C.E. are all ways to be aware and attentive.

Again, it's worthwhile to tune in to how we feel and notice if we're focusing our attention on more fearful thoughts or more loving thoughts. I've often had both skeptical and optimistic voices in my head. I feel quite differently based on what kind of energy I give more attention to. I feel much lighter when I lean more towards the optimistic: faith, hope, and love. Regardless of any drama or situations, I still have choices and I prefer feeling better!

Having an Altar space is another way to focus our attention. When I first decided to create an altar area on purpose, I realized that I had been doing so for years without ever thinking of it as an altar. Maybe you have as well. We often have something similar to an altar on a fireplace mantle or on shelves in our homes. I enjoy the symbolic reminders that support me and nurture my awareness. Today, you could choose to create an altar in a space where you can dance with it in view sometimes. You can choose items that relate to your affirmations, celebrating with gratitude, or anything you want to give extra attention to or appreciate with love!

Looking at my fireplace mantle, I see what I prefer to focus on reflected in the symbolism of items chosen with care. There's an owl figurine. It was a gift from a friend who knows owls remind me of my dad. It represents both intimate friendship and fatherly love. It also reminds me of the time I watched a family of owls through my old bedroom window at my parents' home. The nest was in a palm tree almost touching the house. The family had two adorable fuzzy baby owls. I was still breastfeeding my baby boys at the time. We watched each other nurture life over the week I was visiting. The owl also symbolizes being wise, perceptive, capable and visionary with the ability to see far and well, even in dark times. Next to the owl is a citrine crystal, which is my boys' birthstone. The golden color reminds me of warmth and that the love I have for my children and life is a treasure. Citrine is also associated with prosperity and represents my intention to have a happy, healthy home and family. There are some green candles representing vitality and sacred sparks. There's a Native American flute collected while exploring with my family. It represents the breath of life and the Great Song. There's an elephant that reminds me of a favorite parable about the Divine. There is a card with mandala art and a prayer sent by an online art friend from India. My husband's binoculars are on the mantle for convenience. We use them for watching the birds. They remind me to look closely and enjoy the show of creation all around us. In the center is a sparkling angel. It reminds me of the sparkles in my mom's eyes and Mother Love.

I use a small table in my studio space as an altar. I give it attention any time I feel a desire to update it or shift my attention, such as moon phases, holidays, or seasonally. I don't worry about changing it if I don't feel like it. I don't treat it as an obligation or chore! I don't get caught up in how it 'should' be. I let it support me.

Altars can be used to honor Ancestry, whether physical, cultural, or geographical, as well. My paternal grandmother was adopted by her maternal grandparents when they found out she existed. They went to an orphanage to get her when she was two. I don't know about who her father was or if she was even the correct child. My kids and I did some genetic math after visiting a statue of a distant uncle where we happened to meet a 'long lost cousin.' It's amazing how fast ancestors multiply and connect us! In 20 generations, there are over a million grandparents a person is related to. I'm also thinking of cultural inheritance and being aware how that may affect us. We can honor it and even heal it if needed! I also think of the land I call home. I live in Cherokee territory near the Smoky Mountains. I feel a connection to those who lived here before and learning about and respecting their heritage and presence. I dance with their spirit.

I invite you to give attention to an altar area of your own during your D.A.N.C.E. today. It can be as simple as choosing one thing that makes your spirit smile. Let it be a supportive reminder of energy and intentions to focus on. Trust your inspiration and love.

Refresher: **D**ance, **A**ffirmations, **N**otes, **C**elebration, **E**mbrace

DAY 18

NARRATOR, NAMES,
NEEDS, NOW, NAVIGATOR

Who is the Narrator of the story or the choreographer of the dance you are doing Now? This relates to authenticity and noticing when we are claiming our ability to be the author and narrate our own story or when we are letting someone else do so. Many of us are bombarded by media and advertisements that try to tell us who and what we should be and need. Even the name we're given at birth may impact the stories we tell about ourselves. It was hard for my husband and me to choose and agree on names for our boys!

My given name is Julia. Many people call me Jules. I was called Julie as a kid also. I had too many versions of my name to keep up with. In college, I had even more because some of us chose fake names to use at times! Have you ever done that? I don't recall what mine was. My mom said she chose Julia because she liked Jules, which makes me feel treasured now. So, I introduce myself as Julia or Jules. I looked up the meaning to find youthful or vivacious. I'll keep it! Do you know the meaning of your name? Is it a good fit? I've known adults who've changed their names. You have a choice.

I love a few nicknames I have picked up over the years. There have probably been others I'm glad I've forgotten or never overheard! My boyfriend when I was 14 called me Sweetface (it was when the singer called Babyface was popular). It still makes me smile softly to remember. As a teen, I thought I'd be Precious Jewels if I was a pop singer. I'm not as fond of the word 'precious' since hearing it in *The Hobbit*. I no longer relate it with myself either. I've changed.

It's interesting to me that some cultures give formal names later in life. I've thought about what mine would be if that were the case. My friend, Candace, called me Sunshine when we started to spend a lot of time together. I imagine she probably used that loving term of endearment for other people before, yet it made me feel bright during a time when I was grieving. Her use of that name for me and what it is affirming has influenced the way I see myself and the way that my kids view me as well. I call her Sweetness, which I later noticed is a term my Dad uses. We can encourage and empower people with the names we use. When I dance outside and say, "Good Morning, Sunshine," I think of myself as well. Sometimes, I hear Willie Nelson singing, "Bring me sunshine with your smile."

I think about the wizard stories I've read in which a 'true name' is earned, has power, and is only shared with a few others in deep intimacy and trust. I wonder what my true name might be. I didn't change my first name when selecting a pen name. It was hard enough to choose a last name. It felt as if the pen name I use now was a gift that I chose to accept. It sounds like a more feminine version of the married name I share with my husband and boys.

This also makes me think of name calling, such as Bozo. I notice it a lot in conversations about politicians! What are we affirming for and about others, such as our children, spouses, co-workers, and other drivers, with the words and names we use to describe them?

I've also thought about stories from events in my life and how I've heard and chosen to tell them. I wrote a new version of my birth story. I think of it when I feel a smooth bald dent left from forceps on my head. I was surprised at what came out and how it made me feel warm inside. It reminds me of fantasy novels I enjoy reading. Are there any events in your life you'd like to retell as the narrator?

Here is the revision I wrote as an example:

The Winter King did not want to go to sleep. The chill reached deep into the bones of the forest as the wind blew and blew. The blizzard brought a blanket of snow to cover the land. The fire of life was determined to burn on. The mother was exhausted from so many hours in labor. The home birth was not to be. Mother and daughter needed help to let the new life flow out of the womb. The first carriage (ambulance) was damaged on the rutted road. Another was sent to carry them to a hospital many miles away from the howling hollows of the farm. As the building swayed in the strong breath of the Wind and the mother labored on after more than 44 hours, a babe was wrenched out of the womb to take her first breath. The strong, soft, Sacred Mother could rest while her body, partially paralyzed from the long birth, took time to fully heal. In the ancient Appalachian Mountains, a new Heartlight flickered and sparkled in the frosty depth of the night between February 1st and February 2nd, known in some places as Candlemas and Imbolc, a time when the light grows bright again. The mother gave birth to a Divine legacy of love. The father tended all the fires, the hearth and home, the animals on the farm, the mother and child. Milk flowed forth from the pure well of life within the mother to nourish the newborn girl. Warmth grew in their hearts and the seasons turned as the child and the wildflowers began to bud and thrive... sweet, strong, and vibrant!

Now, that's my version of the story I've been told. The title of this book is another version of the story I'm choosing to live and tell.

Today, I offer a few prompts to consider when taking your Notes:

- ❖ What does your given name mean to you? Do you have a nickname? If so, what does it mean to you? What pen name or true name would you give yourself?

- ❖ Is there an event or story from the past that you'd like to revise or retell from a fresh perspective?

❖ Is there a dream story you'd like to tell about your life? What would the title of your book be?

❖ What do you truly need and prefer right now?

The idea and process of nonviolent communication developed by Dr. Marshall Rosenburg emphasizes the importance of being aware of our own needs and being able to communicate them effectively. We can also be aware and better able to ask and understand what others need in relationships and interactions we must navigate. Some teachers of concepts like the law of attraction may suggest that we 'need' to not feel 'needy' in order to receive whatever we 'need' now. Isn't that a tongue twister? I get the reasoning. Still, after listening to Marshall's audio book about *Speaking Peace,* it seems that many of us experience a bit of confusion when figuring out what our real needs and desires are. Many conflicts seem to arise from such confusion. So, it may be worthwhile to clarify our preferences and needs and those of others to live more peacefully.

Taking time for ourselves to go through the D.A.N.C.E. motions can help us identify our needs by tuning in to our heads, hearts, and bodies. When we have more clarity about what we truly need and prefer, we are better able to ask for and accept assistance if necessary. We may also assist others to get their needs met or set clear boundaries and communicate if we cannot or will not do so.

We can use that awareness about our needs when choosing our affirmations and co-creating our lives. Recently, I've been spelling out and acknowledging some of my needs about community and love while saying, "I trust the right connections and kindred spirits to cross my path. I belong in a sweet Circle of Kindness. I trust my Source. Show me the Magic! Show me the Love!"

I've also been thinking about who is the Navigator in my life lately. My husband and I have discussed the words from the children's song, "Row, row, row your boat gently down the stream..." We've wondered about being in the flow of the great river(s) of life. How and who does the steering? Neither of us prefers feeling like we are trying to paddle upstream! Yet, do we always want to 'go with the flow' in every situation? I think about my thirteen year old boys and remember facing peer pressure. I think about surrendering to Source, Spirit, or the Flow of Life and I wonder about 'free will.' I wonder if we can surrender to the current and help with steering at the same time, such as avoiding rocks, which way to go at a fork in the river or when to take a detour or explore an area on shore.

Are we like navigators finding our way by learning how to use the flowing wind of grace in our sails? I am obviously a wonder filled explorer! I am a wild, wonderfull way finder. I am learning to trust the stars and the stardust within me to help me steer.

I explore and collect ideas, medicine, guidance, and stories from various cultures, religions, and traditions. As a narrator, I revise the language to tell my stories in ways that feel in tune and in harmony with the Great Song I live in. I like flowing, flowery language. It makes me smile and lights up my heart. It makes me feel like a wild flower. I belong in Tom Petty's sweet song about "Wildflowers." This is my true voice. I need to trust myself. I'm learning to co-create and trust the sacred magic within and around me. I trust my voice and vision to flow from a well of wisdom and wonder. I trust the Whole Spirit in me and Source of Life that flows through me.

Your story is yours to live and tell! You are part of a wonder filled web of life. Your vibrant thread in the tapestry contributes to the deep beauty of the whole. You are a marvelous miracle! Is that part of your story? You can explore these ideas and inquiries using your own voice while taking notes, wondering and narrating aloud, or navigating through movements of the D.A.N.C.E. today. The song, "These are the Days" by 10,000 Maniacs comes to my mind. What story are you living Now? Let Your Heart Sing! Bless your life.

Refresher: **D**ance, **A**ffirmations, **N**otes, **C**elebration, **E**mbrace

DAY 19

CONNECTION, COMMUNITY,
CONTRIBUTE, COURAGE

The magic of the creative process is showing up here while writing! Trusting the process and the flow of inspiration led to this idea of Connection and Community for the letter C in our D.A.N.C.E. coming right after the prior section about our stories and needs! Sometimes, we may be able to meet our needs without reaching out for assistance. Other times, we may need to have enough courage to ask for help, whether through affirmations, traditional prayers, or cultivating connections with people in healthy communities. We may also have something to offer and need courage to connect and share it with a community. For example, writing this book is taking courage to trust my voice and trust that it is safe to share so much and trust that others may find value in what I am offering and my willingness to share wondering thoughts and personal experiences.

I tend to be a homebody. It takes energy and courage for me to go out and socialize. Thanks to the internet, I've been able to connect with kindred spirits from around the world in art groups without leaving home! Yet, having a local community can be healthy. Both types of connections have value. Is there something you've been considering trying? Is there a local venue you've wanted to visit or a club you've thought about participating in? Do you enjoy your local library? I love ours! Do you wish there was a local group for something that you could start? Is there an online group that shares an interest you would like to join? Is there a way you might enjoy volunteering locally? I'm glad I made the effort to take an art class at our local folk school years ago! I've since volunteered there, too. It also took a lot of courage for me to take my art to a local gallery the first time, but I'm so glad I did. I think it's also a good example for my kids to see me put my brave boots on.

We can consider the plants and animals as part of our community as well. We are all part of the circle of life and share this amazing planet. I admit that I talk to the plants and animals around our home. I live in the woods and consider the plants and animals as part of my woodland family. I follow the deer trails to go for walks. We share this land. Is there a way you might nurture connections with plants or animals, such as gardening or having a bird feeder? We used to go to a nearby park and an animal sanctuary when we lived in a more urban area. Animal shelters usually welcome visitors and volunteers. Many areas have community gardens as well.

Maybe you prefer smaller groups or one-on-one connections and conversations. Is there someone you've been meaning to call or connect with? I'm not one for talking on the phone much so I am often long overdue for calling dear friends! These days, with video chat options through the internet, we can even have face to face conversations with someone across the ocean or on the other side of the world! It's been great to meet some online friends that way.

One day, I took a video of myself dancing with my reflection in my basement studio door and later shared it on social media. It took courage to be seen in that spontaneous moment with no makeup on while wearing my painting apron and looking into an old door that had stains on it showing up in the video. Yet, that is my life unedited and unpolished. With all the tools out there to edit and enhance the appearance of our lives and images, it feels necessary to sometimes share the spur of the moment, to be more honest, sincere, and intimate with one another rather than only sharing or comparing curated highlights from our lives, to be able to share our pain and disappointments with grace and our joys without shame.

Is there someone you might enjoy connecting and dancing with? It can be anyone, whether alive or not, someone you know or not. It could be your 9 or 99 year old self! I've envisioned myself dancing on stage with Oprah. I enjoy reading poetry with Mary Oliver and Hafiz. My boys and I enjoy Shel Silverstein for silliness. We could even imagine dancing with a fun fictional character like Aladdin's Genie from a children's story or fantasy book. I'm singing along with Robin Williams, "You ain't never had a friend like me!" I also enjoy listening to audio books, especially anything by Dr. Clarissa Pinkola Estés. She is a spectacular storyteller. On days I need to rest, such as during my monthly feminine cycle, I may lay on the Earth while listening to her tell stories. Though I have never met her and she doesn't know who I am, she is a beloved elder to me.

I had an 'aha!' moment when I realized how people like Oprah and Estés have had such beautiful, healthy, enriching influences on my life even though they have not had personal interactions with me. I was finally able to let go of a deep resistance I've had to amplifying my voice and increasing my circle of influence. Once I saw I could do so without exhausting my energy or taking too much time, love, and attention away from family, I could fully embrace the vision. A speech by Dr. Brené Brown about *the Power of Vulnerability* and her personal example as a public figure have also helped me make the shift in perspective, especially since she is also a mother, wife, and phenomenal everyday sort of woman. Realizing how I respect these women, even if I don't always agree with them, helps me be brave enough to share. Now, I trust and allow the Multiverse to multiply my energy and efforts and deliver my musings, medicine, messages, and magic to those who are willing, open, ready, and able to receive and appreciate what I offer. I'm ready to welcome and nurture this sweet sacred Circle of Kindness with courage, faith, and grace.

Is there a sacred circle or community that you've been envisioning in a similar way? Is there a fear or doubt that you might see from a fresh perspective? Ask for divine guidance and wisdom if needed. I think of the song "Life's a Dance" by John Michael Montgomery,

"Sometimes we lead. Sometimes we follow." May we find mentors that bless us and be that kind of mentor to others at times as well.

I also think of this daily ritual as a time to Connect and dance with the Divine, both within me and all around me. Sometimes, I even reach out my hand to say, "Yes, I'll gladly dance with you!" or ask and invite the Divine to Dance with me.

I have talked to 'God' for as long as I can remember. Based on the culture I was born in, I was introduced to the Divine through God as described in the Bible, Jesus, and Holy Spirit. Interestingly, as I've invited Jesus into my life multiple times and learned about the bible, a Loving Wholiness has guided me to feel that there are no divisive conditions and no one is ever left behind or out. Divine Energy keeps coming to the party and dancing with me through many traditions and synchronicities. As I've kept wondering and talking to the Cosmos, I see how unlimited and so much broader the Divine can be than any single religion or entity. I felt inspired to set God free from any one book, story, culture, or tradition.

Now, I have many terms of endearment that I use to refer to the Divine, such as: Sacred Spirit, Whole Spirit, Mother Mystery, Pure Possibility/Potential, Pure Energy, Great Song from the Celtic idea of Oran Mor, Father Flow or Breath of Life, Multiverse, Creation, Gloria, Wind of Change, Grace, Great Spirit, Father Time, Mother Love, Beloved Friend, Source, and Delight. I rarely use terms that have heavy baggage associated with them for me personally. You can use whatever language feels true and comfortable to you. I was just thinking about God and Goddess when I found a way that these ideas feel lighter and healthier to me. I don't think of the Divine as only masculine or feminine. I like this phrase as a union: Yin and Yang. I'm able to visualize the symbol that includes both of those energies as a well balanced Whole. If you have cultural or religious traditions and language that light you up and warm the Whole Spirit within you, use that. If you're not interested in God, then use scientific or humanitarian lingo. Again, I'm reminded of words from the *Desiderata* poem by Max Ehrmann. It is framed in my parents' home and in my home now as well. My dad took it off the wall and read it to my mom after she took her last breath. The words from the end seem particularly relevant. It reminds us that we are all children of the universe, along with the trees and the stars, and it suggests that we be at peace with God, whatever we conceive that to be.

Though I don't think of God as being He or She, I do invite some masculine or feminine energies if I feel drawn to communing with and dancing with that on any given day. Existence is a big mystery to me so I tend to greet it that way. Still, I think of Goddesses or Gods from mythology and traditions who are associated with an essence that appeals to me, such as Sophia for wisdom, Mother Mary as a mother of love, Shakti as life force and flow, Kuan Yin, Buddha, or Christ as compassionate energy, Gaia as mother nature. There are many interesting and bizarre stories humans have told along with the historical accounts. Hopefully, we can share wisdom and wonder through stories and symbolism in peaceful ways.

I admit that I've also thrown fits to God when I've been confused, sad, or angry. I haven't always been at peace with God. Yet, I feel drawn to keep dancing with the glorious mysteries again and again. I feel a Sacred Spirit within and around me. I hope that, whatever you conceive the Divine to be, you can feel the spark of a Divine Spirit within you and enjoy the Dance.

All that took courage for me to share because religion tends to be a controversial topic! Still, it feels worthwhile to be open and honest to nurture community. I hope we can respectfully disagree when necessary and be kind to one another in spite of any differences, including different beliefs and traditions. Now, I'm singing, "Tell me all your thoughts on God" from a song by Dishwalla.

I guess I'll address politics here since that applies to community as well. I'm not democrat, socialist, communist, or republican. I don't think any single political group has all the answers any more than a single religion does. I have been registered as 'independent' since I became old enough to vote when I turned 18. I lean toward local, libertarian, grassroots, and taking responsibility ourselves instead of giving it away. I'm both pro-choice and pro-life in multiple ways.

I hope we can find ways to get along, cooperate more, and thrive in harmony. I know it can take courage to connect and contribute, especially if we feel like outsiders or like we live on the edge. I feel that way often! I love my sanctuary in the woods where I retreat from the world in some ways. I can hear Eddie Vedder singing, "Society… I hope you're not lonely without me."

My parents quit 'good jobs' in engineering and a law office to move back to the land. My first friends were lambs and goats. The hog was a scary monster and the mule threw me off! My dad learned to raise honeybees and shear sheep before starting a successful fence business and moving back to Florida. Yet, my family and I have been trying sustainable organic gardening and permaculture. We're failing when it comes to self sufficiency. I know it can be done better. We have lots of other interests. We'd rather not do it alone even though we appreciate our privacy and personal space. I think of tribes who moved for the seasonal harvests. The way we handle land stewardship, as ownership, doesn't make that so easy. It was interesting to read *The Birchbark House* by Louise Erdrich about the Ojibwe with my boys. Maybe we need to be in tune with nature's rhythms and also have healthy trade practices to fully thrive.

Hopefully, we can find tribes we resonate with, can contribute to, benefit from, and respect.

May we have the Courage to Connect and Contribute to healthy Communities and D.A.N.C.E. with Divine Delight!

Refresher: **D**ance, **A**ffirmations, **N**otes, **C**elebration, **E**mbrace

If the suggestions on any day don't interest you, simply skip that.

DAY 20

ENCOURAGEMENT, EMPOWERMENT, EVERYDAY ANGELS

Do you have anyone that is a cheerleader in your life? My mom was definitely a cheerleader for me before she died. Since then, I've learned to be my own cheerleader. I also appreciate the help of a few friends, some of whom I've never met in person, when I get down or need encouragement or uplifting. I've learned to be more selective about people who surround me when I can. I love lyrics from a song "Turning Wake" by Ayla Nerco that say, "I will dance with the ones who remind me" of my deep and true wholiness. I choose authors, mentors, and artists that feel like they are cheering me on even if I never meet them. It also helps if we are able to love and trust ourselves to fully embrace our courage and power.

What does power mean to you? I've realized that it was something I was uncomfortable with for much of my life. I had identified power with those that wanted to use power over other people to control or manipulate others. While that is one possible aspect of power, I now recognize another side to power. We have a choice and the ability to use power in the opposite way as well. We can empower ourselves and others to cooperate and thrive through our energy, efforts, wealth, and well being. It has helped me to look at people who use power and plenty in healthy, generous ways for examples. Such examples remind me of the potential and help me trust myself to act with similar kindness, compassion, and wisdom.

Are you comfortable with the idea of power? I had to reclaim my power for various reasons, including times when I was physically abused. I know what it's like to feel powerless in such situations. I can recall writing my own declaration of independence. I chose to not let experiences from my early childhood, when I was a victim, continue to define me as a victim in my adult life. I finally decided to stop being in the presence of a past abuser at certain gatherings. I've also chosen to forgive myself for some poor choices I made as a young adult that led to other unfortunate events.

I remember later choosing to shed the weight of self pity, shame, and guilt while writing and adding a feather to my journal one day. I was affirming that I was lightening up. I've also painted an Inner Guardian that represented having the brave strength to stand up for myself. All of those choices and actions, along with learning to trust myself, have been part of reclaiming my power. Have you ever felt the need to do that?

I've also learned about being interdependent and empowering one another since then. I've learned about walking side by side with my husband as we encourage one another while on a path together. We're able to hold hands for part of our journeys and encourage each other to explore our own creativity, loves, joys, and wonder.

I've also found that spending time in solitude with nature can be enlightening, encouraging, and empowering. Yes, Mother Nature is one of my cheerleaders! Sometimes when I feel down, I'll go for a walk. There is a strong old oak tree in the woods by our home that I call my "Catch Me" tree. I love knowing that it will catch me when I let myself fall back towards it! After letting it catch me, I often slide down the trunk of the tree and sit at the bottom letting it hold me. I also go for Listening Walks with Mother Nature. Sometimes, I take nothing with me. Other times, I take a camera or notebook. My kids and I take observation journals outside as part of our homeschool. We write or draw anything we want based on observations and experiences at that moment. I've learned some encouraging messages from Mother Nature! I'm saving those for another book. You could try finding your own strong tree or going on a listening walk to let Mother Nature encourage you. I've even talked to Grand Mother Moon if I need a listening ear when I don't actually want to share something with anyone I know at the time.

I love the idea of having and being *Everyday Angels*. I can remember reading a children's book by that title from the library with my kids when they were little. It touched me more than them at the time! It was about everyday people who encourage and empower others, such as mothers, healers, teachers, friends. I have my own version of the song "Everyday People" by Arrested Development in my head now. I've listened to the *Invisible Acts of Power* audio book by Caroline Myss that touched me in a similar way. In it, she describes various types of generosity and how genuine encouragement is one of the most uplifting and deepest ways to offer generosity of spirit and empower others. It makes me want to encourage kids to share their thoughts, stories, dreams, and color outside the lines as well!

Do you encourage and cheer others on with deep sincerity and generosity? Growing up in a very competitive culture has probably impacted how I've viewed the hopes and successes of others at times. It has helped me to revise ideas I learned about competing. If we can genuinely celebrate the accomplishments, courage, and creativity we witness from others, then we are being truly generous from our spirit and with our loving kindness. We can also choose to view other people's accomplishments from a fresh perspective rather than envy. We can let it be an example of what is possible for us. We can let it inspire us! Looking for ways to cooperate and collaborate with others, especially those that may appear to be 'competition' at first glance, can be healthy. Combining our energy can have even more amazing results!

We can be "better together" as Jack Johnson sings. We can start choosing cooperation instead of competition. Instead of feeding fears, we can harmonize and work together for stronger energy.

I've been putting my brave boots on to ask others to collaborate more. I've received rejections in the process. Most replies if people decline are handled gracefully. However, one time stands out when someone wasn't so nice. I'm grateful for the experience. It made me reconsider my own motives. I'm glad to feel confidently rooted in kindness as a result. I also learned that I don't ever want to make anyone else feel like crawling under a rock! The person eventually apologized and tried to encourage me, which I appreciate.

I've been thinking about how there is only one of me. If there are other people with similar messages to what I offer, then there is more potential for promoting peace and prosperity for the world that my kids and the next seven generations will live in. Let's give proper credit when it is due and let's also pass on love, light, and wisdom. I'd be glad to see any encouraging ideas I share passed on beyond my reach! I'm glad others have similar ideas and dreams. I imagine a Dream Team of people like John Lennon, Rosa Parks, and more current dreamers collaborating with respect, sharing in harmony, building and creating together. I have the song "We are the World" in my head now. In this book, I've mentioned many people whose offerings I value even though I have no affiliation with them. I'm glad to be part of that kind of dream team in my own ways, contribute, and share the soul food. I remember sharing mangoes that we grew on a small tree in south Florida. They tasted like a bite of heaven. I want to share the sweet stuff!

Who can you cheer on, encourage, empower, or collaborate with during your D.A.N.C.E. today? Are there invisible acts of kindness you could do? Even a seemingly simple uplifting or kind comment on social media or a nice note left in a public place for a stranger to find can be a blessing to someone.

Do you need any encouragement today? Do you have any favorite authors or artists that encourage you? I sometimes let oracle cards, poetry, and quotes cheer me on. Is there anyone you can ask and trust to help rekindle your spark if needed? I think of a few friends that I call Magic Mirrors. They are sweet souls who reflect my true beauty to me. Do you have some Everyday Angels in your life? My boys were baking with their Nonni Jane recently when one of them leaned on his brother for a picture. Jane joined him leaning on the other side. The one in the middle said, "I feel like I'm being leaned on!" I started singing a version of the song, "Lean On Me" by Club Nouveau, that I can remember singing with my elementary school choir. Do you have someone you can lean on? Is there anyone you could thank for encouraging, empowering, and cheering you on? I hope you can even lean on this book and Lean On Delight.

Is there some way you could offer a shoulder to lean on or be an Everyday Angel today? I don't mean offering someone pity. I think about the words we use and what we are affirming for others. I want my words and energy to offer strength, be encouraging, and empowering in genuine ways. I may offer a hug if I have no words.

I've also thought of more mystical angels cheering me on. I often walk into the kitchen and see the numbers 11:11 on the clocks. I've started to think of it as a hug from angels and gladly welcome their presence. I've thought of angelic allies whispering to my spirit to "be you to full" while finding the courage to share from my heart.

I've thought I had at least one guardian angel for most of my life. My aunt, Denise, who was my dad's sister, died a few years before I was born when she was just 18 years old. I think my grandmother suggested she was a guardian angel when I was very young so I accepted the idea easily then. She was a confidant growing up even though I never actually met her or heard her reply. Now, I wonder about the idea. I've thought that if my mom could be a guardian angel watching over us, she would choose to be. Yet, I wouldn't want her to hurt for us. I've come across ideas that suggest our loved ones in the mystic have a different perspective so it doesn't hurt them to watch over us. Whether it happens that way or not, I like the idea of a divine loving presence watching over me without judgment, whether angels, my own 'higher self,' or a creative force.

I've experienced a miracle I can't justify according to physics. I had a tiny Miata convertible car when I was in college. I had a long 90 minute commute from Gainesville, Florida to Jacksonville for a job when I was in graduate school. That reminds me, you could even make adjustments to do the daily D.A.N.C.E. in the car if you have a commute like that! It was rush hour on I-95. I was on a ramp to merge onto the highway, which also turned into an exit lane to get off it. All the lanes were barely crawling with traffic. A big rig truck came into the exit lane and hit my little car in the driver's side door. It spun my car sideways along the front of the truck and pushed me. My car went spinning in circles across all three lanes of bumper to bumper traffic. Yet, somehow, I didn't hit any other vehicles! I cannot explain it. It was as if my car was lifted above the traffic while spinning or the other cars were mere projections that had no substance. It happened so fast it made me dizzy. I don't understand how it could have happened the way it did. Somehow, I got over to the shoulder of the road just past the exit. The truck pulled over behind me. The driver said he didn't even know he hit me! There was a dent in my door coming in towards me, but I was still able to drive my car all the way back to Gainesville. It was a surreal trip. I remember the colorful sky as the sun went down during the drive home while I was shaken and left in awe. It makes me wonder if it is a dream or virtual reality or if there's much more to the natural world than we see. I'm singing, "I believe in miracles" along with a children's song about "angels watching over me." Maybe they are!

We can encourage and empower ourselves as well. An online friend shared a comment saying her favorite stories are ones when the girl saves herself. Is there any way you feel a need to save yourself?

Today, I encourage you to D.A.N.C.E. with your own Powerful Sacred Spirit. May we use power wisely, gracefully, and generously.

And it harm none, do what you will. Claim your Divine Power!

Refresher: **D**ance, **A**ffirmations, **N**otes, **C**elebration, **E**mbrace

DAY 21

DARE, DIFFERENT, DRUMMING, DESTINY, DOMAIN, DEEP, DESIRE

Would you like to play a game of Truth or Dare? That was not one of my favorite games growing up! When I think about daring now, I think about daring to be true and daring with discernment. I did stuff that seemed a bit daring when I was younger, such as body surfing at a Metallica concert, racing in fast boats, bungee jumping, and sky diving. I did some stupid stuff, too. I came within inches of going over a cliff on a motorcycle with a stranger. When someone said, "Let's jump off a bridge." I did. Yet, I didn't dare to be me.

I wonder if I was seeking thrills because I felt numb much of the time and didn't value myself much. It has taken way more courage to dare to bare my heart and soul through art and this book than it ever took to do any of that stuff! It feels daring to free myself from concerns of being cool and pleasing others. It feels daring to reach out to others to ask for assistance and invite others to collaborate. It feels daring to homeschool my children. It feels daring to put so much time and energy into writing this book even though it may be a big flopping failure by some standards. It feels daring to speak so honestly and be seen as a middle-aged mom if people actually end up resonating with what I have to say and choose to dance with me! I was more comfortable being physically seen when I had the body for a bikini as a teen, but I didn't dare to show much from the inside back then. I didn't dare to look inside myself much then!

I was so concerned with being popular then. I recall a conversation with my mom as we were moving from West Virginia to Florida. I was in 9th grade and upset about leaving my friends. I wondered how she was happy with few friends. I've since learned how having a family or career to care for impacts the time and energy we have to spend with others. True friendship is about quality not quantity of people or time. We don't have to see each other often to remain friends. Some will come and go. Some stick around through lots of crazy stuff. My college roommate, Michelle, sent a card that says, "friendship is when people know all about you, but like you anyway." We have celebrated weddings and births and been through fogs of grief and depression also. I dare to have deep friendships and not try to please everyone. I dare to be my own best friend.

Do you Dance to the beat of your own Drum, the beat of your own Heart? I have always admired those that seem to genuinely do so! Much of the value I find in the daily D.A.N.C.E. ritual comes from diving deep into my own head, heart, and hopes and being at home with and in myself. I wonder about the idea of destiny and the domains we choose to live in and explore. I wonder how much our beliefs determine our destiny. I think of the song, "I believe I can fly" by R. Kelly. The Wright Brothers dared to believe that it was possible, and they found a way to fly! Tuning in to the body, choosing affirmations, taking notes to get in touch with our inner wisdom and our curiosity, celebrating our joys, and embracing our whole selves are all ways of daring to go deep into our lives and loves. I enjoy daring to be true to myself now. I dare to trust my Sacred Spirit and "have a little faith in me" as Joe Cocker sings!

This also makes me think about how we treat those that seem to 'beat to a different drum' than us. My boys see the world through very different eyes than I do. The eye doctors call it color deficient. We call it color different. Both boys seem able to see some colors, but there are other colors they are unable to differentiate between. Even though we've talked about it, I don't know how they truly see the world. I wonder how my colorful paintings really look to them.

Even lenses in sunglasses can change the appearance of the world. While that's an example of literally seeing the world differently, we may not know much about what conditions lead to other people's perspectives and rhythms. There are so many ways to view life.

I recall a Buddhist parable my boys and I read in the book, *Kindness*, compiled by Sarah Conover. It talks about how differently a group of blind men describe an elephant based on body parts they feel. One man describes a snake. Another says it is a fan even though they are describing the same elephant. The story refers to various ways of interpreting and communing with the Divine as similar to those men. I try to remember this and respect other perspectives about whatever the 'elephant in the room' may be. I try not to assume there is only one right point of view. I caught myself when Jehovah's Witnesses came to my door. I honestly answered a few questions, stopped talking, and offered hugs instead of arguing, which they accepted then left surprised. We may not understand people's views, yet we can dare to act with kindness and grace.

We may also be driven by different things than others or the media suggest we should. Sometimes, there can be so much external noise that it may be hard to know what we truly desire or believe. I invite you to do a little drumming to get in tune with your own internal rhythm and heartbeat. I share a few different ways you could add drumming to your D.A.N.C.E. today: Tapping In, Drum Dancing, or using your notebook like a drum. You can do one, none, or try them all depending on your time and energy.

Tapping In to your body. One day, I found myself instinctively tapping all over my body to get blood and energy flowing. You can sit or stand. I usually start at one end of the body and work my way up or down to the other end of the body while tapping all the way. I tend to start with my feet if I'm sitting down. Use your fingertips to gently tap your feet on both the top and bottom. Continue using your fingertips to tap lower legs, shins, and calves while moving up to your knees. Continue tapping all around your knees and up and around your thighs. While doing this, notice if any areas of your body seem like they could use extra attention or stretching after. Continue tapping up around your lower back and over your belly, sides, chest area, and up to your shoulders. Tap out each arm from your shoulders all around your upper arms, elbows, wrists, and down to and around your hands. Tap gently around your face and up to the top of the head. I especially love tapping all around the eyes, gently tapping on the temples, the eyebrows, and the bone area underneath the eyes! If standing, I usually do the same thing in the other direction starting with the head and working down to my toes. You can do the same sort of thing with a self massage rather than tapping motion. Enjoy your own magic touch! For women, you could do a self breast exam with this as well. I usually start dancing when finished tapping in to the body. Let your body lead. That is my own adaptation of a tapping idea from EFT, emotional freedom technique. I learned the EFT way in a video by Jessica Ortner. You could do it instead if you know it.

I enjoy adding Drum Dancing during the day sometimes as well. While doing the physical movement of your D.A.N.C.E., you can gently drum on your body with your hands. You can drum on your belly, heart, legs, or whatever feels good. I'm singing along with Rod Stewart, "Oh, the rhythm of my heart is beating like a drum."

I also love drumming while finger painting! You can do something similar without the mess or add some color if it sounds like fun to you! Even the colors you choose can reveal something about your deepest feelings. Before taking notes, you can use your note book as a drum, using your hands to create your own beat for a while. You might tune in to something deeper in your head or heart that can come forth in your free flowing notes. Let your heart sing.

Dare to D.A.N.C.E. to the Beat of Your own Drum, Your own Heart Beat today! Tap in to any Deep Desires. Dance with Delight!

Refresher: **D**ance, **A**ffirmations, **N**otes, **C**elebration, **E**mbrace

DAY 22

AUDACITY, ACKNOWLEDGE, APPLAUSE, APPRECIATION

Give yourself a big hand! Have the audacity to acknowledge and appreciate yourself today. Many of us tend to be more comfortable noticing what we admire and appreciate in others. What if we can be our own best friends today?

I love when words have subtle aspects and multiple meanings that can lead us to consider things from more than one perspective. Appreciation means being thankful. It also means recognition of worth and increase in worth. Acknowledge means to accept the existence of and to recognize and admit the truth of something.

Today, let us recognize our own deep worth. Let us accept our own existence. Let us admit the truth that we are all marvelous miracles. Let us accept that, by existing, we are worthy of life and love and delight. Let us see value in our lives, loves, wonders, joys, hopes and true selves. Let us be lively and kind. Let us respect ourselves.

I hope that you can see yourself with Loving Eyes today. I've been working on this myself while writing this book and working on the promotional and bonus videos to share with it. While editing the videos, I've seen myself slowed down and paused in many awkward expressions. It's been a gift to be able to see myself through loving eyes rather than focusing on any perceived flaws! For instance, I've been able to think of my double chin as a double smile instead. I'm able to see the true beauty of love, reverence, wonder, and delight shining on, in, and through me. I invite you to look at yourself with loving eyes today. Instead of focusing on any perceived flaws in your appearance, look for the deep, pure beauty of your sparkling spirit. Do or celebrate something that lights you up from the inside out and feel the delight shining through you.

To write this and make videos, I've had to be willing to be seen and give up some of the anonymity I've enjoyed so that I can share this much of my life, head, heart, and soul. It takes courage to do so while being aware that there will likely be critics. I decided I wasn't writing it for the critics. I'm having the audacity to write it for me, for the life and inspiration that flows through me, for any kindred spirits that may appreciate it, for creation and community. We can decide that we aren't living for the critics either! I'm thankful for a quote about a bird singing because it has a song, rather than having answers. It's been attributed to both Maya Angelou and Joan Walsh Anglund. That quote has helped me to gain confidence and trust my song. I hope you can let your heart sing, too!

Do you know the parable about the talents? At least one version of it is shared in the bible and attributed to Jesus. It's challenged me in the past. The story refers to a person who buries their 'talents' and others who multiply them. Talents could refer to gold or abilities. I didn't feel talented for most of my life. How could I bury what I didn't have? The art that has flowed through me in the past decade has pleasantly surprised me. I gave up art for too long. I thought I couldn't draw and wasn't talented as an artist. It has taken time to exercise my creative muscles and explore the process to strengthen my voice. Now, I can view the art that I create with loving eyes!

When I tried to multiply money I invested in the past, I lost much of what I didn't bury. Thankfully, I'm able to see the parable about talents with a fresh perspective now. I'm thinking of talents as gifts or blessings. I notice many gifts in my life when I think about what I'm grateful for and love. I see reverence, wonder, kindness, joy, and nourishment are all gifts. Looking at it like this, those gifts or 'talents' seem like great things to multiply! It feels healthy to share seeds of joy, soul food, spirit medicine, and sweetness that have the potential to promote peace and prosperity. Money can be a tool to use that way. I think of the words presents and presence. Maybe our presence is a present! Your presence is a gift. I don't know how or why, but you are here now. You are present. You have the magic of life flowing through you. You don't need to have any answers to be talented. You have gifts and presence to share. You have a song!

While doing your Notes portion of the D.A.N.C.E. today, please write what you Appreciate and Acknowledge about yourself. You could even give yourself an Award if that feels satisfying! Leave comparison in the waste bin. Don't waste your time on it. This has nothing to do with comparing, popularity, self pity, or arrogance. It is about love. Reconsider what love means if needed. Give yourself some "R-E-S-P-E-C-T" today! Don't apologize for who you are. While apologizing can be healthy, I've noticed that I was affirming "me so sorry" way too often just because I wasn't able to please everyone. I'll spare you the tune it plays along with in my head if you don't know it. I'm changing it to "me so lovely."

I encourage you to write a Love Letter to yourself today. Take your time with this if you can. You are worth it. Dig deep. Find all of the sparkling treasure within you. Trust the Sacred Spirit within you. You are wonder full and delight full. You are Divine. Fall in love with yourself. Let that love fill you and radiate from you. It blesses those around you as well. I've also noticed that self love and self respect are sexy! I've experienced the evidence in my marriage.

The more self love I feel, the less self conscious I feel! Self love and respect can enable us to be generous and kind rather than arrogant, which seems related to insecurities to me. Seeing ourselves through loving eyes may help us to see others and the world through loving eyes also. May we live in love, not with anything else specific, rather living in a state of love. I wonder if self love and respect may lead to being responsible and able to care for ourselves well and have healthier communities with others who are able to do the same.

You could leave little love notes in your home, books, bags, or car to find later. I love finding them on something that I've used as a bookmark. I just found one that said, "trust the treasure within," written in my own handwriting on the back of a postcard. It was great timing right after I'd been questioning the value of my voice and messages! I also enjoy mugs with my art on them. I was feeling overwhelmed one day as I was stepping out to dance. Then, I saw the words "I belong" on my coffee cup before I started dancing and enjoying the roses about to bloom. It was a touching reminder that I belong in this magic moment! I love that my boys also use the mugs and get messages like "I see the pure light within you." I recall a suggestion in a health magazine to write reminders in the cabinets or fridge about diet. I'd prefer to find compliments in the pantry like, "You're beautiful just the way you are" or "Every little thing she does is magic," inspired by the Billy Joel or Police songs.

Let Your Heart Sing. Serenade Yourself! You are a "Masterpiece." An old boyfriend gave that song by Atlantic Starr to me. Now, I'm singing it to myself. You can, too! Even if we're works of art in progress! Some of my favorite paintings are ones that don't quite feel fully finished. I sometimes leave them that way on purpose like an invitation to imagine how it could evolve at any given time. There is beauty in the process and joy in the journey. Love yourself right here, right now. You're "a work of art it's true."

Please write yourself a Love Letter today. Dance to your own sweet Love Song. Applaud yourself at the end of your D.A.N.C.E!

Refresher: **D**ance, **A**ffirmations, **N**otes, **C**elebration, **E**mbrace

PS. This is a great tradition to do on birthdays or Valentine's Day. I've declared it a self love day. As James Taylor says, "shower the people you love with love," including you!

DAY 23

NAKED, NON-JUDGMENT, NOTHING

Have you noticed that we're getting more bold and intimate during the D.A.N.C.E.? I'm glad the letter N and this idea happen to come after yesterday's activity! If you've skipped to this step out of curiosity, you might want to visit the prior page first. I want you to bring a healthy dose of Self Love to this step.

Yes, today, I invite you to get Naked during your D.A.N.C.E, both physically and symbolically. Let's dance with both vulnerability and courage today. Let's be liberating and set our Spirits free!

I loved the results when I typed the word 'non-judgment' into an online search engine to see if I was spelling it correctly. Though the spelling search was inconclusive, since I found it spelled more than one way, the headlines and highlights from the first page of links were inspiring. I think it was an audio speech by Ram Dass that helped me notice how much mental judgments were impacting me years ago. Today, I want to encourage you to be non-judgmental with yourself. If judgmental thoughts come up, witness them and let them drift away or use the bubble popping idea from day 15. Please choose love, sweet love today for yourself.

Are you comfortable with your naked face and body? I don't wear make-up as much anymore even though I used to sell it once upon a time. I still enjoy dressing up and getting fancy on occasion. I still use make-up that way and if I'm feeling very vulnerable. Yet, I'm more comfortable being seen without it now. I'm also becoming more comfortable and less ashamed with my own naked body in solitude. I'm remembering core worth and presence aren't the same as our appearance, clothing, possessions, past, cellulite, or scars.

In 2015, I hosted an online course about putting brave boots on and living with brave hearts. One of the suggested activities was to dance naked. I did it myself before I would suggest it to anyone else. I closed my bedroom door and took off my clothes (not on camera!). I thought about symbolic hats, roles, beliefs, expectations, judgments, and perceptions to 'take off.' Ayla Nereo's song, "Show Yourself" to know yourself comes to me. I invite you to do this in a safe space. Keep a pair of brave boots on if it helps. Nothing else!

If that's too much for you or you don't have an appropriate safe space, you can do a symbolic strip dance without taking clothes off. As suggested above, 'take off' any obligations, roles, expectations, judgments, etc. to strip down to nothing. What hats are you tossing in the air? Graduation cap, taxi driver, chef, nurse, guard, knight, jester, crown, cowboy or girl, police, athlete, janitor, dunce, guru, halo, witch or wizard? Notice how you feel as you take it ALL off. Do you feel relief and lighter when taking any particular thing off? Do you feel like you want to hold on to anything or put it back on?

These can be clues to help guide our lives from the inside out. We can go skinny dipping for an invigorating cleanse and still return to our responsibilities after. We may altar some things before putting them back on for a better fit. We may be able to leave some things off or make other arrangements to let someone else help. We may enjoy the warmth of specific stuff to put back on. We might play dress up and try on some new styles as well.

I think about when my boys were in the hospital and the rest of the world seemed to stop turning to me. My husband still had to go to work, but there were other things we stopped doing. No one really expected us to attend many events given the situation. What if you don't need an excuse to respectfully say no sometimes? This has been a big change for me since I tried to be a people pleaser for a long time. I've been learning to set healthier boundaries and choose priorities for myself and immediate family rather than letting others do so. I'm being brave and bold enough to disappoint others and recognize other adults are responsible for their reactions. It's been an adjustment for me and people I let pressure and manipulate me previously, even if they didn't realize it or it just felt like it to me. I don't want to be pressuring others that way either. I'm taking more responsibility for my choices, commitments, freedom, and worth.

I appreciate the value of doing a symbolic strip dance every once in a while because it helps me get underneath it all to return to my original divine nature, which is my Presence. Let us get to the true treasure buried under all of the hats and labels. Let us see that our bare being and presence is worthy of life, love, and joy here and now, not based on how our bodies look, what abilities we have, how we dress, or what we own. Let us see this applies to everyone.

I remember a sweet little children's book that I used to read with my boys called *The Gift of Nothing* by Patrick McDonnell. I adore children's books. You could give yourself this gift by taking even just a few minutes to be still, with no need to be anyone specific or do anything in particular for a few moments, and Do Nothing! You could skip the rest of the D.A.N.C.E. today if you want.

Thinking about Nothing or 'no thing' reminds me of the Buddhist teachings about detachment. The idea of detachment is something I resisted for a long time. I tend to be a hugger! Over the years, I've had a few experiences of forced detachment that caused me to reconsider the idea. In 2009, our old home was broken into when we were not there. The thieves took my jewelry boxes. There wasn't a lot that had much monetary value in them, but there were several sentimental things. There were foreign coins from travels, newspaper clippings, friendship bracelets, other jewelry from child-hood and my parents, the first necklace my husband gave me, a few inexpensive pieces of jewelry collected on travels, broken bracelets and earrings that were missing mates. The jewelry boxes had been gifts from family. The stuff that likely disappointed the thieves as junk held lots of love and value to me. My husband's guitar that I bought him when we first started dating was also stolen.

A few weeks later, I arrived home from the grocery store with my boys to find the front door had been busted open! I had no idea if there was still anyone in the house. It was scary. The police came again and searched the house in case anyone was inside. Nothing was missing that time. Maybe they left as we were pulling in. We felt so violated twice in a month. The stolen stuff was never found. As it turns out, I rarely miss it unless something makes me think of it or I want to wear one of the pieces of jewelry that wasn't broken. Thankfully, my husband could afford a new guitar. I've learned not to dwell on it. I don't use jewelry boxes anymore though!

When the neighbor's house was broken into while I was writing this book, it prompted me to forgive those people who broke into our home so long ago, say a prayer, and set myself free.

I've thought about how much baggage we tend to lug around, both physically and symbolically. It was interesting trying to fit stuff in a single backpack for a four week trip around Europe. I remember my Grammie saying they didn't have closets when she was young. A few wall hooks were enough to hold their clothes. Back when I was listening to survivalist stuff, I put together what was called a 'bug out bag.' It's like a camping bag that I keep in my car in case we ever need it in the middle of nowhere. My kids liked watching Les Stroud's show, *Survivor Man*, and learning about that stuff. It does put necessities into perspective. I think about people moving west with covered wagons and nomadic tribes from the past.

Now, I wonder if sometimes holding on to stuff can weigh us down in more ways than we might realize. When my mom died, it was hard to go through all of her stuff. I saved some of her clothes even though they didn't fit me. I thought I'd make a quilt someday or use it for other craft projects. I've recently started donating much more stuff, including mementos and clothes from old life roles and sizes! I've taken truck loads to donations and some to the trash. So far, I've no regrets! It feels liberating to shed some stuff!

I notice if I fear losing stuff, it feels like it starts to own me instead. I don't want to feel like a slave to stuff! Realizing I don't really need that much has helped to free me from having a scarcity mentality, hoarding, and fears of being robbed or having nothing. I still prefer to live a rich life, full of opportunities, joy, beauty and nourishment for my family. I have a full house and my original artwork is piling up! I feel blessed right now. I also feel more content and confident in my ability to thrive in various circumstances. I feel lighter.

Facing the death of loved ones has also forced me to detach, at least from the presence of their physical bodies as I knew them. I've learned to view detachment from a new perspective that has helped me understand it differently even though that word still doesn't feel quite appropriate to me. I've reconsidered the lines from Janis Joplin's evocative song claiming that, "Freedom is just another word for nothing left to lose." It always made me wonder.

Now, I'm learning to be both free and full at the same time.

Maybe it has to do with being present and living in the moment, accepting and appreciating the gifts of now. I think it also has to do with confidence and trust or faith. In the past, I hid some stuff so well for fear of losing it that I can't even find it myself now! Maybe that's what the parable meant about burying talents. I don't want to hide my blessings that way anymore! I feel fortunate to have plenty to lose. I have no desire to lose it, except maybe a few pounds. I am enjoying my home, family, art supplies, creative practice, books, and lots of other stuff. I'm also grateful to feel less afraid of losing most of it than I used to be, which gives me the courage to live more like I have nothing to lose!

I'm reminded of a quote I rediscovered in my own handwriting. It was on the back of my high school senior picture. I was surprised at the wisdom in it that I don't recall having at that time in my life! The quote was by Jan Glidewell. That's a fun last name. I wonder if it was chosen on purpose as in to 'glide well.' The quote talks about not clutching the past so tightly that we are too full to embrace the present and the gifts of life right now! We could do the same thing with plans about the future. Maybe the sweet spot is feeling free to glide well with the wind of change and feeling fully blessed with all the memories, all the dreams, and all the gifts right here and now.

It hasn't always been easy, but I'm learning to trust the "Wind of Change." I sometimes sing along in the morning to the Scorpions' song, "Take me to the magic of the moment... in the wind of change." I've also named a painting after the song. The painting shows part of a naked woman standing with a tree. She is bowing to the divine in herself and others as the wind and seasons change.

Today, I invite you to do a little strip dance, either physically or symbolically. Get naked, strip down to nothing, no baggage, no judgments, no obligations, no past regrets, no worries, nothing to lose. Choose what to leave off and what to put back on with care. I have the "Hakuna Matata" song about no worries from Disney's *Lion King* movie playing in my head now. Probably not your typical strip dance song, but it sounds good to me!

Set your spirit free! Be "Uncaged" as described in the song by Zac Brown Band. That song makes me want to be outside with the wild birds, which makes me feel like a "Wild Thing" letting my heart sing. I keep singing my own version of that song by The Troggs.

Bare your beautiful Brave Heart in the D.A.N.C.E. here and now. Feel a fire in your eyes as Starship sings about being "Wild Again!"

Refresher: **D**ance, **A**ffirmations, **N**otes, **C**elebration, **E**mbrace

If the suggestions on any day don't interest you, simply skip that!

DAY 24

CLEANSE, CHANGE, CHANTING

If you're going in order through the daily activities and ideas, this is flowing on with the wind of change that I mentioned yesterday and mental cleansing. When I became more aware of the thoughts in my head, I noticed how stereotypes and cultural stories sometimes influenced my initial thoughts. I wanted to make a change.

I would not have considered myself prejudice. I had an interracial relationship when I was a teenager. I loved him and his chocolate skin. After receiving disapproving looks and comments, I thought we might have a solution to racism if people mixed genes together so we'd eventually all be the same color. I feel differently now. You can love and mix anyway you want, but not for that reason. We'd lose so much beauty in the variety of features. I recall a hair stylist, who was coloring my hair, describing it as dishwater brown when I was in college. It made me feel dull! I love a colorful world. I love my family's blue eyes. I'd enjoy an even more colorful bouquet of people like many different kinds of flowers or vibrant paints. Some people would probably still differentiate based on beliefs, status, or abilities even if we all physically looked the same anyway.

I notice sometimes when I hear people placing so much emphasis on a particular group or color to defend separately, it can feel more divisive. While diversity and variety may refer to similar ideas, I get different feelings from a focus on division, such as shame, disgust, judgment, accusations, or us versus them separation, that doesn't feel truly encouraging or empowering. I'm shedding guilt I felt for being born a middle class 'white' woman (though I'm a mutt and had no flushable toilet as a young child). I don't think we lift others up by putting ourselves down. Focusing on variety and acceptance feels inclusive, as if inviting us to come together to cooperate and harmonize like in the song by Stevie Wonder and Paul McCartney. "Ebony and ivory living together in harmony" sounds great to me.

I feel very fortunate to have worked with and enjoyed people from many different backgrounds and ethnicities when I lived in south Florida. At one job, only a few of us in the company were born in the United States. I was with co-workers from Venezuela, Pakistan and India on September 11, 2001. I saw how it affected them also. I love learning about other cultures, traditions, and places and connecting with a variety of people. It's not as easy to do in some small towns. It was a blessing to get to know families with Muslim backgrounds and Hindu backgrounds to see that we have a lot in common with hopes, dreams, joys, and love for our children. Even though I realize there are some extreme cases of people from most cultures that may be less loving and kind, I am grateful to have had the opportunity to be friends with such a variety of people!

Still, I've noticed how assumptions sometimes pop into my head unintentionally about people I encounter, such as "she looks like Barbie so what problems could she have?" She had a lot of heart aches and trauma when I heard her story. This relates to the non-judgment idea from yesterday focusing on thoughts about others instead of ourselves today. I was surprised at initial presumptions that came to my mind one day when I was behind a vehicle at a stop light. Once I became aware of my thoughts, I chose to change them instead of presuming stuff about the strangers in front of me.

I've probably been the one being judged at times. I drove our old pick-up truck from south Florida to the north Georgia mountains by myself. I accidentally cracked the windshield while trying to fit my husband's piano bench in the passenger seat. I put tape on the windshield until it could be fixed. Our homebuilt chicken coop was in the back of the truck with our three pet chickens inside it! I put a tarp over it so the feathers wouldn't fly. I drove with the windows down because the air conditioning didn't work. I looked like a real wild woman with windblown hair. You could hear the rooster crow when I stopped at a rest area. I remember the looks and comments from a few men who saw me walking back to the truck. I wonder what the drive-thru person at the Chik-fil-a restaurant would have thought if the dear rooster had crowed right then!

I didn't actually think of that story when I was at the stop light as presumptions popped into my head uninvited. Yet, I still wanted to change my thoughts and energy, whether the car was a clunker or a Corvette, even though the strangers in front of me probably didn't know or care what I was thinking. I think I chanted the word 'love' to myself or started singing, "Love, Sweet Love." I don't want to judge people based on the vehicles of our physical bodies either. I want to feel more kindness and good vibrations for all of us.

Yet, there have been times I felt otherwise. I remember when my gut felt alert to a van driving slowly past me. I was pushing my kids in a double stroller. I trusted my instincts to take a different path to walk away from the van and made a phone call to tell someone. It is natural and necessary to use instincts and awareness of potential consequences to use our 'good judgment' and make those kinds of choices. Admittedly, watching too many movies about kidnapping probably doesn't help! Hopefully, we can use wisdom gained from experiences and still choose a voice of love most often.

I remember another time I felt a similar concern about someone suspicious in a group situation. A man seemed to be taking photos of other people's children. A few parents voiced concerns to the park rangers. I also imagined a loving, protective shield, kind of like a giant hug, around the rest of the group of strangers, especially the kids, at the national park. I don't know if my feelings were accurate, yet I trusted my need to choose and focus on a particular energy. I looked directly at the man and focused on loving energy. Doing so gave me more confidence in the situation and reduced my anxiety. It helped me lean in to love and respect for life rather than fears.

Sometimes, I visualize the shower water cleansing my thoughts and carrying them away. I've also danced outside in the gentle rain. I've imagined the rain cleansing any old wounds and showering me with love, blessings, and a pure flow of life. I've taken a drink from rain drops on a plant. Part of cleansing for me has been about changing beliefs and ideas that didn't feel healthy, whole, and loving. That makes me think of *The Power of Myth* book by Joseph Campbell and the *Mythbusters* show that my boys love! Maybe we can bust our own myths if they're not serving us in healthy ways.

I've adapted traditions when I felt inspired to. I've imagined letting old patterns or ideas flow down the drain after taking a bath. I did my own sort of baptism in a nearby mountain lake. It symbolized purification and rejuvenation when I chose to trust my own pure, Divine nature and the presence of a Whole Sacred Spirit within me.

I have also done a cleansing ritual with fire. In autumn, as the trees were releasing their leaves, I used a sheet of paper to write what old habits or beliefs I was releasing. Then, I added it to an outdoor fire. That reminds me of an idea I've heard mentioned about *Change Me Prayers*. I haven't read the book by Tosha Silver yet. It's on my list. The title is thought provoking. I like the idea of Divine assistance and focusing attention to change ourselves and our lives through prayers. It may sound contradictory after talking about loving and accepting myself as I am now. I've learned to be more comfortable with contradictions, changes, and being within a creative process.

I've also used fire to burn smudging sage and palo santo wood for cleansing myself and our home. I especially like to do this before having visitors while saying a blessing such as, "May we see beauty in one another. May we reflect the Divine spark in each other. May we respect one another and enjoy our time together with love." I wish to focus on the inner light, life, and sacredness in others more often, especially with my family and as a wife and mother. I prefer to encourage and feel love, vitality, and joy rather than dwell on any criticisms. However, change may be needed if in abusive situations.

I've found chanting to be an effective way to shift my energy and change my thoughts when it feels necessary. Similar to choosing affirmations, choosing something for chanting can also nurture our confidence and ability to trust ourselves and life. There are many Kundalini yoga mantras you could use. I've appreciated those and use them sometimes. I prefer using my own language and intuition more often. I sometimes sing or chant "Omma" or "Amma" while dancing. I pronounce Omma with a short sound for the letter 'o' as in mom. I learned that Oma means grandmother in German. It's not a word I grew up knowing or using. Since my mom died, I've noticed a desire to feel more connected to a Great Mother Spirit and Energy. The way I choose to say Omma has a similar sound and vibration to the Sanskrit Om, which is commonly chanted during meditation. It also sounds like "Amma," which means spiritual mother and is a name used for a woman known as the hugging saint. I love hugs and the idea of embracing Mother Life!

Sweet synchronicity sure seems to enjoy making me smile. About a month after writing the paragraph above, I was at the park with my family. Some people in our local community are painting rocks and leaving them in parks and on hiking trails for others to find and hide again. We found a rock that said, "Hugs Heal." My son, Evan, said, "That sounds kind of like your mantra, Mom." He knows how much I love hugs throughout the day! My other son, Drew, said, "It's a momtra!" I love how the painted rock prompted the conversation, which is a blessing to me now. I'm glad my boys think of me that way. I love sharing this memory with them. I don't recall having discussed mantras with them before, though we may have. What mantras would you like others to associate with you?

I sometimes choose a song to sing and chant instead of a word or sound. There have been encouraging song lyrics repeating through my head recently. The words "don't be afraid to make a sound" from the song "Sacred Breath" by MaMuse have magically played through my head while writing this book! The lyrics "we are all bright" from "Synchronicity" by Rising Appalachia and "Shine on" by James Blunt have also been in my head. Musicians can totally be muses and messengers to inspire, encourage, empower and connect us. I've had amazing moments when songs come on while painting that sing right to or through my art and heart. That brings me back to the idea about soundtracks for our lives. My kids and I refer to some songs as "sticky songs" because they get stuck in our heads so much! That's sort of how a chant or mantra is used purposely.

Let's change any stinkin' thinkin' and change our tunes if needed. The words "no pain, no gain" popped into my head, which I hear in someone else's voice. Others have passed that idea on to me. I choose to change it. I'd rather follow my bliss as Joseph Campbell suggests. I also hear the phrase, "it's all good" in my friend Kane's voice. I'll keep affirming that! It reminds me I'm part of a bigger mystery beyond my understanding. It reminds me of the serenity prayer about having the wisdom to know what we can or cannot change. We may not be able to change others or change certain situations, but we do have the option to change our own minds and moods. I think of the songs "Free Your Mind" by En Vogue and "Man In the Mirror" by Michael Jackson. I'm starting with me.

Have you ever done a *Mad Libs* page? It's a game with stories that have blanks to fill in for missing words. My boys love it. We could use our notes to write any thoughts we prefer to change and cross out some words to make blanks to fill in like a *Mad Libs*. I love adding a playful touch to this kind of stuff. It helps me lighten up!

Changing our routines can also help us change habitual thoughts or patterns and bring fresh ideas and insights. Going on vacation is great, but simply going a different way to get somewhere we go often or eating unusual food will do. We recently had a homemade pizza night. One of my sons doesn't care for many of the usual toppings so he enjoyed adding corn, boiled egg, and raisins to his. He inspired us to make a delicious fruity dessert pizza, too! The boys also enjoy finding exotic fruit at the grocery store. The food, especially Thai, is one of the few things I miss from city life. It's fun to explore different languages, too. We learned that "Mangia!" means eat in Italian on pizza night. We learned French words when visiting Quebec, Canada, where my ancestors once lived. My dad often said, "Bon appétit!" to start dinner when I was younger. I've seen the difference it makes in liveliness and conversations with my family to try new things or explore new places. I enjoy living where seasons change after living in Florida. I find it refreshing! Even re-arranging furniture is a way to change our surroundings. Are you familiar with the Danish idea of "hygge?" It's similar to comfort or cozy contentment. You could make a hygge corner in your home.

Going to a new club or church is another way to try new things. I've been meaning to visit a local garden club for years. My parents made some great friends through a garden club in the Keys. Their beautiful tropical garden was featured on the club's garden tour a few times. As a child, my parents let me go to church with anyone that invited me. We lived in rural West Virginia so there weren't as many kinds as there could have been. Still, I found it interesting to visit different ones with friends. There was only one that was scary amidst them. I've enjoyed learning about more spiritual traditions since then, including taking my children to some grand Christian cathedrals, Buddhist temples, Japanese gardens, and cliff dwellings at Mesa Verde. I'd love to visit Glastonbury and the Alhambra also.

How could you change it up a bit today? If you usually do a fast dance, you can slow it down or vice versa. If you usually listen to music, you could change the type of music, use instrumental music, or dance without any music today. If you don't usually have music playing, you can dance with music today. You could try a new kind of dancing you've never done before. I haven't tried Riverdancing yet even though I have Irish heritage. Have you? I remember trying polka dancing once at a festival. It was fun! You could also change the location of your dance today. We put chairs in the creek to cool off and get a fresh perspective sometimes. It's invigorating! Is there some place different you can go to take notes even if you don't do the rest of the D.A.N.C.E. there? You never know what you might discover. When evenings grow warmer, I enjoy dancing outside as the sun goes down. I recently added some hanging solar lights to a tree in our yard. I was dancing under the tree when I noticed little droplets of condensation sparkling on the lights and felt low leaves tickling me. I'm easily amused. I find wonder all around me when I take the time to look closely. You can change your perspective by zooming in or looking at something from upside down today!

You could also enjoy a cleansing dance in an indoor shower or outside in the rain if the weather accommodates. Let yourself be showered with a pure flow of life sustaining water. You could go for a swim somewhere. You can drink a refreshing glass of water. "¡Salud!" as the Spaniards say for good wishes and cheers to good health. Now, I'm thinking of Latin salsa dancing or "Livin' la vida loca" with Ricky Martin. Oh, that's one of those sticky songs! How about adapting the lyrics from Santana's "Smooth" instead to sing, "I'm just like the ocean under the moon." The Divine flows within and through all of us. Let it flow, let it flow, let it flow.

I invite you to chant during your D.A.N.C.E. today. You could repeat "Omma" or any sound or word you like while dancing. You can add some harmonious energy with a song. You can sing "I feel good" like James Brown or add lyrics from a song like "Shine" by Collective Soul. I've been singing my own version of the lyrics to chant, "Let the light shine through me." If you have a specific song that lifts and lightens you up, you can use lyrics from it as a mantra to chant. You can make up your own "sticky song" if you wish! I wonder what you will choose to chant during your D.A.N.C.E. today. Let Your Heart Sing!

Refresher: **D**ance, **A**ffirmations, **N**otes, **C**elebration, **E**mbrace

DAY 25

EXPLORATION, EXCITEMENT, EASE, EYES OF WONDER, ENERGY, EARTHING

As a mom, I've felt at times that I want to protect my kids from the world. Yet, I also want to encourage them to explore this amazing planet, the wilderness and the wonder, the variety and the vast possibilities, their own imaginations, hopes, joys, loves, and lives. Becoming their mom helped me to open my arms and open my heart more to life, to be more curious again, to liven up and lighten up, to express myself, and to Explore with Eyes of wonder.

I remember a conversation prompted by my kids asking about the purpose of life. We wondered together while talking about learning, experience, exploration, expression, play, joy, love, and being. I think of our approach to homeschooling as earth or life schooling, though more exploring than schooling. We are required to cover certain material and also see the necessity of preparing our boys to function within a particular economic environment. We also focus on topics, such as trust, kindness, cooperation, respect, creativity, vitality, joy, and confidence, that aren't on standardized tests. I'm glad some parents and teachers do so with kids in school as well. We try to encourage curiosity and let wonder be a guide for our explorations. We sprinkle our home with books, tools, art, natural collections, games, and anything else that may provide enrichment or spark an interest. I do the same with my email and what I follow on social media to sprinkle that with stuff I might enjoy exploring.

I haven't been a student of *A Course In Miracles*, yet I've appreciated my friend, Corinne Zupko, sprinkling my inbox with quotes from it and information about it that gives me tastes of it to consider. I've done the same thing to sprinkle this book with lots of food for thought. Explore the ideas that excite you or spark your wonder or boost your energy or make you feel at ease, and leave the rest.

I needed to 'unschool' myself in some ways as John Holt describes it. Many of us experience some conditioning, or what Don Miguel Ruiz refers to as domestication and John Taylor Gatto describes as "dumbing us down," while we are growing up! I went through a time of feeling rather numb as a young adult following a path that others expected me to and going through the motions to get an education, degrees, and a job so I could pay my own bills. I saw the movie *Dazed and Confused* many times during college. Those words fit that time in my life too well! I wasn't really Excited about much. I wasn't Exploring ideas and activities that interested me. I wasn't Expressing myself. I didn't feel at Ease with myself or life. I didn't allow myself to feel much at all. I did get a decent job, but I still let work, 'happy' hours, and alcohol numb me for a few more years. Many college friends remember it more fondly. Maybe they paved their own paths more or had a deeper sense of worth than I did.

I get the meaning of being 'wasted' now. I'm not wasting more of my time on blame, shame, or regret. I've finally learned to trust and stand up for myself. Maybe trust, ability, and liberation are my gifts from those experiences. I once heard a woman reply to, "what do you do?" with "I'm finding myself." I had to do that, too. Having a loving, supportive partner helped! I'd rather encourage our children to trust their own Excitement, Ease, Energy, and Eyes of Wonder to Explore without going through the haze that I did if possible!

After feeling adrift, untethered, and lost for a while, I'm glad to feel more embodied for now. I appreciate the gift of this sensual body and having my feet on the ground, even though I have my head in the clouds often as well! It feels like a healthy balance. It's easy to do in the mountains where I live. Some days, I can literally stand with my bare feet on the Earth and be in the clouds at the same time. I gladly explore and appreciate the presents of this planet. I'm also open to the wonder, the mystical, pure energy, and wholiness!

I feel fortunate to be so alive and awake now! It feels better to be high on life to me. I know I'm lucky I survived some of the stuff I did and situations I was in as a young adult. I wish my brother-in-law would've been able to fall in love with life and been around to meet his nephews instead of experiencing drug addiction that led to his death when he was only 26 years old. I've found that loving life helps me to accept things like that even though I don't understand.

Somehow, I'm able to feel more open to love and life through the cracks in my heart. It feels like a way to honor life, and the lives of loved ones that died, to lean in to Explore with Eyes of wonder, to feel Excitement, to open and share my heartlight through creative Expression, to open the gifts of life on this Earth, to lighten up and celebrate the sweet joy, to be at Ease with myself, my body, and the mysteries of creation, to D.A.N.C.E. with divine life and delight!

Today, I invite you to Explore the wilderness, both inside and out, with open Eyes of Wonder. What do you see? What have you been feeling and experiencing recently? Has anything been weighing you down? At times, I've had a heart heavy with grief, whether I was grieving an opportunity, an idea, a home, a pet, or a dearly beloved person. I've also carried weight that might not really be mine to carry through compassion and empathy. I've experienced dis-ease in my body from the weight of the world and my own heavy heart.

Do you see any areas of stress, heaviness, worry or dis-ease when you look into the wilderness of your life? Is there anything you need to escape? Is there a healthy way you can? Escape can be healthy sometimes, such as from concentration camps. Even taking dance breaks from an office or an office chair at home can be a great way to have a short escape to loosen up and liven up.

After our neighbor's home was broken into, I had a dream that I came home to find the thieves in our house. Somehow, I noticed that it was a dream, and I could choose to escape or change the situation. I decided I could just make the thieves disappear since it was a dream. Poof! They were gone. I don't know how to do that so easily in our daily lives. Still, I'm willing to try with my choices, especially regarding worry, paranoia and anxiety. I watch much less television, certain kinds of movies, and sporting events than I used to. I don't want too much sarcasm and violence in my life. Is there anything you can choose to make disappear in a healthy way in your life? I'm glad that I managed to escape the smoking section many years ago before having a family! I also enjoy escaping my own head with interesting fantasy worlds and novels sometimes.

To me, the word 'Enlighten' is about feeling lighter. Is there some way you'd like to lighten up?

Is there something that makes you feel at Ease and in joy? We can explore while choosing some affirmations by noticing what excites us. What makes you want to sing "I'm so Excited" like The Pointer Sisters? If anything immediately comes to mind, explore that! You could also ask yourself what you are curious about to explore that more. What interests you? What makes you sing, "Oh, I wonder, wonder, wonder..." or say "What if?" Explore these ideas while choosing your affirmations and writing your notes.

I like to explore life and myself through inquisitive writing, intuitive art and expressive dancing. You can explore ideas and questions in your notes today or use the body to express yourself through dance and movement. You can think of how expressive some indigenous tribal dances are for inspiration. I sometimes feel like I tell stories when I'm dancing. I've even added face paint before! I remember witnessing a lovely young woman explore her emotions through an expressive dance when she was facing a potentially severe medical condition. It was in a bible study group many years ago, yet I still remember because it touched my heart so deeply without words.

If possible, it's also wonderful to have some space and solitude in nature while writing and dancing! If that's not convenient, then you can do this step without dancing at the same time or in addition to dancing privately. I feel fortunate to live in a rural area with woods between our house and our neighbors' homes. This makes it easy for me to step outside my front door and dance in my front yard without anyone watching (unless my boys or husband get curious or a delivery person happens to pull up the long, gravel driveway). The important part of this step is to find some Earth you can touch with your bare feet! Please be aware of risks from extreme temperatures and don't spend much time doing this in freezing weather. You can wait for warmer weather to do this if needed! Let yourself be in tune with the rhythm of nature's seasons.

It can provide such a strong foundation of support to know and trust that Mother Earth is always there holding us. I first came across the term and idea of *Earthing* in the book by that name by Ober, Sinatra, and Zucker. I think I only read a few chapters, yet the activity has stuck with me for years. I've been doing something similar most of my life and maybe you have to. I spent my early childhood in wild, wonderful West Virginia where I was barefoot outside much of the time. I later moved to the islands of the upper Florida Keys where I was barefoot in "Mother, Mother Ocean" or on the coral sand often. I hope you have some place accessible you can enjoy being barefoot on the Earth today or sometime soon. It's great if you're able to dance barefoot on the rich foundation that is our home, especially if it's covered in soft green moss or bright sunny dandelions. Watch out for bugs and bees though!

It always feels good to me to reach down towards my bare feet and place my bare hands on the Earth forming a flowing circuit with my body (from hands to Earth to feet). Let the pure Energy flow! I do this as part of my daily D.A.N.C.E. most days if weather allows.

If you're familiar with or curious about Shakti, as life force Energy, you can explore that today as well. Let it flow freely through you.

Did you unearth anything while exploring your inner wilderness that you'd like to give to the Earth for composting? I've given disappointment to Mother Earth to transform. Do you need to be reminded how miraculous and nourishing the Earth is? Is there any place where you can pick something straight from the Earth to eat?

Sometimes, I lay down on the ground or on a picnic blanket on the ground while watching the trees or clouds or closing my eyes while 'Earthing.' It's a great way to rest if needed. Let yourself be held, whether while dancing, standing, sitting, or lying down. You can use your Eyes of Wonder to look more closely at the vastness and intricacy in a tiny spot. My kids reminded me how to do this when they were little. It can take a really long time to go for a hike when investigating every bug! We still turn over rocks or decomposing wood to watch during observations. We usually try to leave them as we found them after. The mosses, lichen, and other stuff in our woods often remind me of coral reefs I've seen when scuba diving!

You might even like speaking to Mother Earth. I remember feeling depleted and desperate one day. I was feeling empty. I sat down in the front yard, closed my eyes, and shared my thoughts and despair with Mother Earth, trusting that I wouldn't be criticized, pitied, or ridiculed. When I opened my eyes again, I noticed all of the edible plants right there under my nose! It felt like the Earth was easing my concerns and giving me an encouraging reminder that I am indeed provided for and cared for. I accepted the gift and ate some clover and dandelion leaves. I let this Earth hold me, feed me, and flow through me. I remembered to love life and I let life love me!

I've noticed that the Earth's rhythm impacts my Energy. Even if we live in a tropical place, the amount of daylight still varies with the seasons. When I started to observe my own energy and moods more, I noticed that my energy changes with the seasons. The more I feel in tune with and trust a natural rhythm, the more I've been able to flow with it rather than fight it. I've learned to retreat more during the dark hours of winter. To my pleasant surprise, this book started forming near the winter solstice when I was taking time to catch my breath and made more room for rest and reflection.

This book is rooted in the rich soil from many years of exploration, experimentation and expression through art, journaling, blog posts, and creativity without knowing where or how or what seeds would grow. I had the first draft of this book done by my birthday, in the beginning of February, when the earliest of spring buds started to awaken. Inspiration kept flowing so I kept adding to it. I thought it might be done by Spring Equinox, but it kept growing. I sensed it growing with the seasons and blooming to grow fruit. The trees painted the woods green. I picked strawberries while adding more sprinkles to the book around Mother's Day. We picked cherries as the book grew into June. The date of publication and presentation turned out to be June 21st, the summer solstice where I live.

I love the symbolism associated with the timing. It feels so in tune with a natural rhythm. The summer solstice is the day most full of light, a time when life is in full bloom, and some sweet fruit is ripe and ready to gather, eat, share and enjoy. It's when my family picks blueberries and mulberries. I love how prolific and delicious the berries are! It's a time of harvest that continues into fall. I also love the symbolism and the balance with the winter solstice on the other half of the Earth. It's a time of darkness to tend the inner gardens and fires, a time of planning what seeds to grow, a time of rest and renewal. It's also the time when the daily light starts to grow again.

Today, I hope you can Explore and dance with Excitement, Eyes of Wonder, and your bare feet touching the Earth! I hope you are blessed with a "Peaceful Easy Feeling," like The Eagles sing about, while you stand on this sacred ground.

Let yourself D.A.N.C.E. with Pure Energy and Delight!

Refresher: **D**ance, **A**ffirmations, **N**otes, **C**elebration, **E**mbrace

If the suggestions on any day don't interest you, simply skip that!

DAY 26

DEDICATION, DEVOTION,
DEFINITION, DIVINE, DELIGHTFUL

What does dedication mean to you? I sometimes reconsider the meanings of words, look up definitions, and choose how I define them for myself. After choosing dedication to write about here, I looked up the word. The aspects of the definition that stood out to me were about giving time and energy to something because it is important to us and doing something in order to honor or express affection for someone. Then, I looked up devotion wondering if it would be much different than dedication. The points I noticed for devotion were about a feeling of strong love and about the use of time, money, and energy for a particular purpose.

At the beginning of this book, I wrote a dedication. I invite you to do your own dedication during your D.A.N.C.E. today. You could dedicate your dance as a tribute or offering to a specific person(s), something, to yourself, or to life in general. I once did a dance as a tribute for an owl that crossed my path. I found it shortly after the breath left its body. I recorded the dance with an old camera to share with a few kindred spirits whom I thought would honor and appreciate it. I often feel the trees dancing with me while dancing outside and have dedicated time to that. This entire book feels like a kind of devotional dance to me. So, I made a promotional video about it into an offering and dedication in honor of the inspiration, Sacred Breath, the beauty and blessings in life, and divine Delight!

As I've shared before, I sometimes feel that I am dancing with my mom, whether her presence within and around me or her memory. I usually feel that I am dancing with the Divine within and around me as well. Typing that prompted me to look up the definition of the word divine since I use the word so often. I was reminded how much even a subtle difference in interpretation or perspective may influence what a word or idea means to me and what the supposed same word and thing may mean to someone else!

I'm drawn to aspects from the definitions for the word divine that refer to sacred and delightful. What does divine mean to you? What does sacred mean to you? What does delightful mean to you? To me, Delight could be ecstatic, exciting, and expansive! Delight can also be strong, soft, serene contentment and deep inner peace.

I think of Delight as the Sacred Spark within me.

Thinking about the word and energy of the Divine, I remember an email from a publisher. The subject line suggested writers consider their 'crutch' words. I didn't read the message. I get the impression it was something to improve. It made me think of 'divine' as being one of my crutch words. I think it's a pretty great crutch to lean on! Maybe it's worth considering what our crutch words are. They may define our lives in ways through the power of our words. I prefer words like sweet, sacred, magic, and delightful. What about you?

I've become devoted to dancing with Divine Delight and the whole morning D.A.N.C.E. enritchual. Every step has influenced my daily energy and outlook. It makes my days more rich and magical! For example, here's a glimpse into a day: "I feel the wind chimes echo through my body with the wind in my breath. I let myself just be for a few magic moments. I feel myself opening and blossoming. I see raindrops sparkling like jewels all around me. I remember how fascinating this wide, wild wonderful world is! I am a facet of this wholiness, which makes me feel fascinating, too. I breathe in the blessings." That was after checking a week's worth of homeschool work and before tending to kid's injuries and getting in a pickle! A giant dill pickle jar broke flooding out of my car on my flip-flops in a parking lot. I just had to laugh and admit life is a mess sometimes, too! I can choose the story of a mundane, middle-age mom trying to pay the bills or the life of a magical, magnificent, mystic momma sharing my gifts. I'm dedicated to the second version of the story!

Dedication and devotion also make me think about Determination or Discernment. I have mixed feelings about determination. Maybe it's because everyone in my house has a strong stubborn streak! I'm learning to use discernment to determine how I use my energy. I prefer loving dedication and devotion to guide my determination.

The first thing that pops into my head when I say the two words dedication and devotion is the song "Walk of Life" by Dire Straits. What are you dedicated and devoted to in your Walk of Life? What do you honor and love? What makes you feel delight full?

I'm also reminded of the song dedications that I used to hear when listening to the *American Top 40* radio show each weekend when I was growing up. You could dedicate a song to someone else or to yourself today. I've done this by sharing links to a song in emails or through online comments to dear friends and family. I've offered dedication posts to whole communities after a big event as well. I dedicate the song "Beautiful" by Carole King to you today!

I encourage you to write your own dedication(s) in your notes. We can dedicate our lives the way authors dedicate books. I think the legacy that matters most is love rather than anything else we do or create. I also invite you to look at yourself in the mirror and see the Divine sparkling in your own eyes! Define yourself as Divine. You are beautiful. Remember to give yourself a big hug.

Dedicate this D.A.N.C.E. with Devotion. Dance with the Divine… Dance with the DeLight inside you!

Refresher: **D**ance, **A**ffirmations, **N**otes, **C**elebration, **E**mbrace

DAY 27

ADAPT, ATTITUDE, ARRANGE, ACTION, ABLE, ACCORD, ALIVE

"Get into the groove" like Madonna or "go your own way" with Fleetwood Mac. Adapt and Arrange the Activities corresponding to the letters of the D.A.N.C.E. to be in Accord with your Ability and rhythm! Do what makes you feel Alive so life continues to flow through you with ease. Let the ritual be fluid and flexible to change.

My boys often ask if they can adapt some instructions from the few school books we use, especially when it comes to writing. One of them recently asked if he could write about a fictional sporting event instead of an experience with a traditional sport. He likes a video game that uses a motion sensor where the players dodge unusual objects like bowling balls. I'm glad he was able to shift his attitude as he started getting more animated and excited explaining it to me. I said, "Yes! Make it fun and enjoy the process!"

When I remember to do that during chores, I feel myself lighten up also! If I put on my happy mix of music, I'm able to start singing, dancing, and having fun while folding laundry, cleaning the kitchen, canning salsa, or cooking dinner! I'm glad I have a big kitchen since it's also my dance floor. If the D.A.N.C.E. ever starts to feel like a chore to you, please Adapt it! That's part of the reason I share so many ideas and activities in this book. Change it up to enjoy a change in Attitude! Anyone else singing along with Jimmy Buffett?

We may also need to adapt our language to better reflect what we are trying to communicate and how we prefer to live. I invite you to make up your own new words like I have with 'enritchual' and 'presentce.' You could also create your own acronym and routine ritual with other letters if you feel inspired to! Here are some of the many ideas I've explored for keeping this ritual fresh and adaptable. Feel free to add your own ideas as well!

D   Dance, Dedication, Dream, Draw, Dare, Darkness, Desire, Devotion, Definition, Domain, Drumming, Divine, Deep, Donate, Destiny, Discernment, Dimension, Discovery, Do, Diversity, Decide, Delicate, Delicious, Different, Delightful

A   Affirmations, Attraction, Action, Angels, Altar, Awaken, Awareness, Attention, Authenticity, Audacity, Acceptance, Acknowledgement, Art, Alive, Able, Aim, Ask, Act, Am, Arrange, Agree, Accord, Awesome, Adore, Appreciation Amma, Alone, Aid, Adapt, Animal Spirit or Animal Totem

N   Notes, Nourishment, Nurture, Narrator, Navigator, Naked, Non-Judgment, Notice, Nature, Night, New, Nap, Nest, Namaste, Native, Negotiate, Neutral, Novelty, Nutty, Nice, Nursery, Neighbor, Now, Noble, Needs, Names, Neat, Net

C   Celebration, Communion, Create, Connection, Care, Circle, Confidence, Commitment, Compassion, Chanting, Change, Cleanse, Collective, Contentment, Ceremony, Concentrate, Cycle, Circulation, Continue, Choice, Customize, Complete

E   Embrace, Enjoy, Exotic, Empower, Encourage, Express, Enlighten, Equilibrium, Expectation, Exhale, Ease, Excel, Exploration, Environment, Encompass, Earthing, Engage, Entertain, Elemental, Eat, Elevate, Envision, Experience, Ecstatic, Essence, Enough, Expansive, Energy, Enritchual

Most days, I stick to the basic steps keeping it sweet and simple. Still, I love to explore and experiment with all sorts of enriching activities and ideas when I have the ability, time, energy, and desire. Since ritual is about enrichment to me, I wanted to include plenty of rich possibilities for adapting the basics. Do what makes you feel light and alive! Thinking of the word Alive has me singing, "I'm Alive and Well" with Dave Matthews and Kenny Chesney. It also makes me think of the sticky song, "Stayin' Alive" by the Bee Gees.

I suppose my song references are too cultural or generational for many people. I don't know what songs are currently popular on the *American Top 40* list or internationally. You could Arrange a happy music mix of your own! You could dance with the minion cartoon characters and Pharrell Williams singing along to, "I'm Happy" or other muses and music that brighten your attitude. I go through phases with theme songs that make me feel good. The song "So Alive" by the Goo Goo Dolls has been playing in my head lately. Would you like to sing along? "I'm so alive! I'm so Alive!"

What Actions make you feel so Alive? While it's usually worthwhile to think before acting, it's often necessary to take some action also. Taking action doesn't mean I focus on productivity the same way it is addressed in business schools. I tend to protect my family's time by not scheduling too many activities on our calendar. None of us seem to be social butterflies by nature so I stopped pressuring my kids. I didn't always handle it this well. I remember being exhausted and frequently talking about how busy we were. It even seemed like something to be proud of. I've since learned busy isn't the same as lively. It amazes me how we have so many conveniences in modern life and can still be so constantly busy. Some people may genuinely prefer to be very active or get cabin fever if home a lot. Decide what's healthy for you based on your own preferences, personality, and abilities. I enjoy flexibility, free time, and "wide open spaces" as the Dixie Chicks sing. I've learned to pay attention to how I spend time and what I need to do or enjoy doing. It enables me to have time for the actions that fuel my inner fire and nurture vitality.

Action might even be pausing to watch the birds or the clouds go by! I've noticed that when it comes to action, there are some tricky lines between persistence, patience, and procrastination for me. If I was more patient with the writing process for this book, it may not get finished. If I had rushed it more, it wouldn't be such a gift to me or anyone else. When the first printed proof copy of this book arrived, I was dancing and singing, "What a Feeling!" I was initially thinking of the song about dancing on the ceiling. When I went to confirm Lionel Richie sang it, I found lyrics for the Flashdance song by Irene Cara, which are also appropriate! It says, "Take your passion and make it happen." I'm glad I kept taking inspired action while also doing my best to go with and trust the natural ebb and flow of the process, including adding a bit since the first proof.

I've learned if I don't ride a wave of enthusiasm when it's flowing, I rarely catch it again. It's a delicate dance to balance between the rests and the making of the music! I relate well to both turtles and hummingbirds. At times, I seem to be in slow motion. Other times, I seem to be zooming. I learned hummingbirds almost hibernate when they sleep. Maybe we need times for hibernation, too! I'm learning to adapt and adjust more according to natural rhythms at different times. It can be challenging if we need to coordinate with others or work in a corporate structure. I love having flexibility. My family has made some big adjustments and choices to arrange our lives this way, yet my husband's job still sets our schedule for now.

If you've been reading through the book all at once, as I sometimes do with this kind of book, it may be time to take action. If you've been very active already and feel like you need a break, take it!

Today, I invite you to make your own joyful music mix playlist or choose a single song that makes you D.A.N.C.E. with Delight. Adapt the steps if desired to brighten your Attitude. Re-Arrange things if needed. Take Action. Liven Up and Let Your Heart Sing!

Refresher: **D**ance, **A**ffirmations, **N**otes, **C**elebration, **E**mbrace

DAY 28

NIGHT, NEXT STEPS, NEW

As I've shared, I usually like to do the basic D.A.N.C.E. ritual in the mornings. I love to take spontaneous dance breaks throughout the day as well. Any time of day is a great time to invite delight to dance with us! I especially love to dance at night when the moon rises in the evenings just after sunset, which happens when it is full. It's a marvelous time for a "Moondance" as Van Morrison says! If you happened to start this book on a full moon and have been going steadily through each day in synch with the moon's phases, then it will be an almost full moon for you today! Even if the moon isn't out, it can be wonderful to do a little Dancing with the Stars, the ones in the night sky rather than the ones on television.

It's only been over the past few years that I've become more aware of moon phases and how my feelings and energy are affected. If you haven't given much notice to it, you might find it interesting to be more attentive to your feelings for a full monthly moon cycle. Our bodies are made up of so much water that the moon may influence us as it does the tides. I hope you'll find this D.A.N.C.E. enritchual worth doing for many moons. So, you could start noting moon phases and your feelings during your notes going forward if that appeals to you. The *New Moon Calendar Journal* created by April Miller McMurtry is a tool for observations and learning about this.

I tend to do most of the D.A.N.C.E. ritual basic steps at night just before bed, in addition to having my magical mornings.

I slightly adapt the steps represented by the letters for Night:

Dream

Affirmations

Notes

Celebration

Embrace

I think of beginning and ending each day with a simple and sacred spiritual practice of this kind as a way of hugging the day! I love to give my days a loving Embrace of rich appreciation. I usually Celebrate the day by taking Notes in a gratitude journal at night. I call it my Joy Journal! It isn't the same notebook that I use in the morning, though I often have that on my nightstand as well. My Joy Journal is usually fancier than my notebook. I made the one I'm currently using. It has a fabric cover that feels good to hold and touch. It has pretty scrapbook paper inside. It feels like a present that holds more gifts inside as I note what adds **D**elight to my days. I usually take just a few minutes to **A**ppreciate, **N**otice, **C**elebrate, **E**mbrace, and love life. The nightly steps can be that easy!

I let life love me! That statement feels like a welcoming invitation. I remember listening to an audio book by Robert Holden and Louise Hay called *Life Loves You.* I very much appreciated the wisdom in the book. Yet, I haven't always felt and believed that life loves me. Making a subtle adaptation to let it feel more true and acceptable to me and acknowledging that I can allow, invite, and welcome love in has made a difference in my ability to believe it. "I let life love me!" I sing along with the Beatles, "Let it be. Let it be."

That's the kind of adaptation I was referring to on the prior pages. Nuances like that can really impact our feelings. So, I reiterate the suggestion about adaptation here in the Next steps. Choose your own New phrases, words, or language if needed in order to Let Your Heart Sing and Let Life Love You! I've obviously made up my own new capitalization rules for emphasis while writing this.

I might do the practice described on day 5 to give love to my cells and body while I'm falling asleep at Night. It can help me relax and ease into rest. I had a beautiful vision after dancing outside with many fireflies adding magical light around me one night. I imagined cells sparkling within me like fireflies full of healthy divine delight. I don't know how, why, or when thoughts like that work to heal. My mom was trying similar things yet her body didn't heal before she died. She said she wasn't afraid to die, but she really wanted to be here to see her grandkids grow up and she felt like she still had so much to live for! I don't understand the mystery or how we know when to hold on or when to let go or if we have much choice. Yet, I'm aware of a placebo effect and powers of belief and imagination, whether for our wellness or not. I appreciate that I feel better when choosing and affirming loving thoughts for my body.

I enjoy 'Dreaming' with visualization and intention as I go to sleep as well. I've done this since I was a kid. Now, I focus on feelings I prefer like joy, love, ease, harmony, and gladness. I've visualized how delightful I saw this book being. I've welcomed you with open arms to dance with me! I've seen my family exploring in areas we visit when I give presentations. I've felt joy as something helps my boys to see a more colorful world. Before moving here, I imagined being surrounded by nature and living in a comfy home. I imagined a water view. We built a little zen pond by the front porch for now. I fell in love with this land. I'll do the same elsewhere if the time comes. I'm glad I can enjoy "Living in the Moment" as Jason Mraz sings and also living my dreams. I'm a dream catcher and a dream weaver! I prefer to live in a sweet dream. I might visualize a 'happy place' as I drift off to dream, such as where the mountains meet a sparkling sea. I might also focus on what I'm thankful for already.

I invite you to add the Nightly Steps and give this day a big hug. Dance in the Moonlight if that sounds like fun. Weave your own Delightful Dreams during your D.A.N.C.E. tonight. Sweet Dreams!

Refresher: **D**ance, **A**ffirmations, **N**otes, **C**elebration, **E**mbrace

DAY 29

CYCLE, COMPLETE, FULL CIRCLE, CEREMONY, CONTINUE, CONTENT, CONFIDENCE, CHOICE

I love watching the sunset. I love watching the moon rise. I also love watching the sunrise when I happen to be up early enough to see it. Isn't it wonderful how our days and nights gently turn with such grace and beauty? I love the changing seasons and how there are times for rest, times for planting, times for tending, and times for harvest. I love the full creative process. I love seeing something grow and become Complete and then Continue to touch others.

I am grateful for the proliferation of ideas and inspiration that flow through me. Yet, it means I usually have many unfinished projects and lots of videos to be edited. We have to choose how we spend our time and energy. What to continue and complete? I'm learning to follow the curiosity, pleasure, love, and delight when I can.

I hope you have loved dancing with the moon for a full Cycle! It takes approximately 29.5 days for the moon to complete one full lunar cycle from new moon to new moon. If you've been going along each day with me, whatever moon phase you started on will be coming around again today or tomorrow. Thank you for sharing this moon dance with me! If you're going at your own pace, that's great, too. Keep going your own way and enjoy the D.A.N.C.E!

I hope you Continue to be enriched! I hope you feel Confident and

Content. I've thought about the word and idea of contentment a lot. I recall a conversation I had a long while ago with my husband when I was sharing that I thought my mom was a good example of being content. It seems that being content isn't always encouraged. It might be seen as 'settling' for something or being complacent, lazy, or apathetic. Yet, I think there may be a subtle difference and kind of deeper peace related to being truly content and confident. I wonder if the emphasis on competition in some cultures may be influenced by our level or lack of confidence and contentment. It also seems that if we are more content, we may be harder to sell to. I wonder how much advertising may impact us. If we are confident and content with ourselves and our lives, we are probably less likely to feel a need for the latest weight loss or anti-aging products or some other item, such as jewelry or a car, that is supposed to make us more attractive or happier. That includes books like this, which may be why I never intended to write this kind of book! However, I've experienced and seen so many others striving for approval and attention or feeling insignificant or overwhelmed that I'm willing to share ways I've found to feel confident, content, and complete.

I hope you remember you have many Choices each day regarding how you feel, think, act, react, live, and love. Whether or not you continue this daily ritual, I hope you can choose to Live and Dance with Delight in some way! I invite you to Celebrate Completing a full length moon cycle or possibly many more days if you've been taking your sweet time to flow through the suggested steps and ideas. If you have a favorite outfit or adornment, you could play dress up and wear it today. Have your own ceremony to celebrate. Dance with deep beautiful Confidence. Let your Delight shine!

Honoring a full cycle, you could incorporate circles into your daily D.A.N.C.E. in some way. You could do this by making circles with your neck, shoulders, arms, hips, feet, or whole body. You could do the hokey pokey if you know it. You could try spinning like a kid getting dizzy. You could imagine you're a Sufi whirling dervish or an indigenous hoop dancer or use a hula hoop. You could do twirls. Do you know the song, "Twirl me" by Wildlight? You could put it on. I love sparklers for adding magic to an evening. You can dance with sparklers and sing "Celebration" by Kool & the Gang. I did that while finishing the book! You can say "Cheers!" with some thing bubbly, whether sparkling water, cider, or champagne. I enjoy sparkling water with a small splash of rosé wine and rose petals.

I also love how drops in water make rippling Circles and watching the splashes and ripple effects! Is there someone you think would enjoy this D.A.N.C.E. ritual? You could invite them to dance with you so this book can have sweet ripple effects! You could pass on this book when you're done or give them another copy. You could invite them over to share the basic steps and dance together. You could twirl each other! You could have a dance party!

While working on this book, I drew an oracle card about a Lantern Dancer. It was about letting the Divine be the light that guides us. I've kept it in my heart while writing. When I made a video to share about the book, I was blessed with a magical morning. I couldn't have made the video so magical if I'd tried to on purpose! The sun was shining bright. Lots of circles, prisms, and sparkles of light are dancing with me in the video. It's like a lantern dancer was with me! You can imagine yourself dancing with a Divine Light Keeper who guides and blesses you. Feel the delight shining all around you, on you, in you, and through you. I was inspired to turn the video into a tribute offering. I created a nature mandala to bless the book. It felt like a sacred ceremony to celebrate the presents and presence and to prayerfully let it go with love. It was powerful and peaceful. Trust the Divine light and inspiration that guides you from within. Create your own sweet sacred ceremonies to celebrate your life.

As a cycle comes to completion, another continues. I hope you feel confident, continue to celebrate life, and choose to keep dancing. Let the Delight within you take the lead. Your life is a love song.

Refresher: **D**ance, **A**ffirmations, **N**otes, **C**elebration, **E**mbrace

DAY 30

END, EXTRA, ENOUGH, EXPAND, ENRICH, EVERYDAY, ESSENCE

What if we treated Everyday as a celebration? This ritual is a way to do that to me. I sometimes skip a day or a few for various reasons. I definitely notice when I do! I notice a shift in my energy if I start my days in a rush or in a rut. I've been a bit extreme with emotions for most of my life. When I'm feeling good, I'm flying high on life! If down, it's felt like drowning or being buried in depressing muck. The ideas shared in this book have helped me handle emotions in healthier ways. Getting up or outside and dancing if I start to feel heavy or low is a great trick for lifting myself up. You could lean on this book like a cheerleader now that you've reached the end. Open it at random for encouragement anytime. That's what I plan to do!

I love doing the basic D.A.N.C.E. steps almost Every day. I usually keep it sweet and simple, even when I enjoy having plenty of time. The simplicity makes it easy to stick with it. The sweetness makes it something I love and look forward to. That is Enough to keep me enjoying it and feeling Enriched every day. The other ideas shared throughout the book are Extra ways to Expand and explore when we have time, energy, motivation or inspiration to do so. I hope I've presented the ideas in ways that feel both easy and enriching!

While one cycle Ends, another day begins. A few days after I did a mandala blessing ceremony for this book I found myself singing, "even endings can be sweet" from a song "Glorious" by MaMuse. If you haven't seen the mandala video, it's on the resources web page. It's pretty sweet! Wrapping endings in love like that can help us embrace a new dawn. I hope you find the D.A.N.C.E. enritchual worth doing with your own rhythm Every day when you feel like it without pressure. I hope it may be a present in your life for many moons. I wonder what the world may look like if we all started our days with an enlivening and enriching delightful D.A.N.C.E. party!

I've thought a lot about having and being Enough and also being Expansive. I thought about that more when I noticed how deeply rooted and unhealthy my ideas about appetite and ambition were as I mentioned earlier. I wonder if sometimes I felt hungry and empty because in a way I didn't feel like I had or was Enough. I wonder if I was afraid of aspirations because I was afraid of having and being "too much" or being seen as greedy and fat. It seems crazy to read those sentences and say I was afraid of not being enough and being too much at the same dang time! I was uncomfortable with the word abundance because it made me think about having too much to eat and weighing too much. Yet, denying myself a deeper feeling of fulfillment led to drowning my desires with alcohol and eating comfort food to try to fill the emptiness and satisfy the hunger!

I started thinking of the word abundance as "a bun dance" instead so I could smile at it. I was a teen when the song, "Baby Got Back" by Sir Mix-a-Lot was popular so that's what "a bun dance" makes me think of. Yes, I fit the song and dance along! Yet, after adding humor and revising my view of abundance, I still felt discomfort with similar ideas about plenty, greed, excess, and richness. I was more comfortable with the word Enough than Extra or Expansive.

Exploring the ideas more through journey work, writing, inquisitive painting and art, I've been able to heal in many ways. I've thought about ambition as aspiration and looked up the word aspiration. It's another word with two meanings I love. In addition to referring to hope and ambition, it refers to the act of drawing breath! Hence, having healthy aspirations is part of being alive. I've journeyed with myself using suggestions from the book *Avalon Within* by Jhenah Telyndru. I've danced with the little girl inside me who felt like she had to be small, starve, hide, or hold her breath. I've witnessed the generosity and the empowering actions that are possible if we allow abundance, plenty, extra, wealth, and richness to flow through us, both to and from! So, I no longer deny having a healthy appetite or appropriate ambition rooted in hope, kindness, vitality, and delight!

I have always loved to give, whether hugs, encouragement, physical gifts, financial support to charities or in healthy exchange, such as purchasing organic food. I'm grateful to have the options and glad to support the farmers, who in turn nourish me. Yet, I spent years feeling unable to afford to do and support things I would've liked to because of my financial situation. I still gave encouragement and support in as many creative ways as I could think of. Now, I see I didn't have a healthy balance with giving and receiving, reciprocity, and replenishment. We must breathe both in and out. I'm learning to give where it's truly appreciated and to gladly accept gifts as well.

I finally see how being more expansive can enable more sharing of abundance, nourishment, richness and the flow of life! I see my appetite and ambition are not just about me or my body or bank account. I'm willing to give and also receive. I've reconsidered what a healthy appetite is. I no longer try to starve myself, not physically nor energetically, experientially, or financially. I have a very healthy appetite for life and love. I enjoy sharing the wellth! I've been told that I'm a great gift giver for years. Yet, I felt that I had no obvious talents. Now, I am able to see the value in that aspect of my spirit and embrace it. I see that I am a presenter, one who shares beauty, blessings, and presents that I receive and have to offer.

I've learned that I can be content with having and being Enough right here and now, and I can also be Expansive at the same time! This also applies to our creative projects. While writing this book, I thought it was done multiple times. Then, inspiration would strike again! I'm so grateful for every message and memory that flowed forth. Still, I find myself saying, "enough is enough... for now." I can expand it in another edition if inspired to eventually. I recall hearing the suggestion, "done is better than perfect." I think about being an imperfectionist while focusing on Enough, Excellence, and Expansion. I'd rather celebrate and share this than suffer from analysis paralysis or strive for elusive perfection that prevents me from publishing this book. I originally envisioned this being a more colorful book with images and artwork scattered throughout. When I saw how much it would cost to print in color, I chose to offer the first edition this way to give it the potential to reach more people affordably. I decided to trust that the message itself is Enough and beautiful enough as it is without dressing it up and making it more expensive. I've tried to lead the D.A.N.C.E. by example. I kept on dancing most days while writing. This book is the result of doing, dreaming, and daring combined. May it be enough and enriching.

I had an expansive shift while dancing one night with fireflies in a gentle rain. I asked for cleansing of anything needed. After an hour dancing and wondering aloud, I felt limits shattering, whether self-imposed or accepted from fear, guilt, or shame. I think of the video for Lindsey Stirling's song, "shatter me," with a girl in a glass globe. It felt great to shed and shatter some limits to expand my essence!

I feel lighter when I accept that I am both Enough and Expansive here now. I am able and open to experience all of the beauty and blessings life offers to me. I love seeing and sharing the beauty, joy, richness, and magic all around me and within me! I embrace my Muchness! I am a phenomenal Everyday woman. I am not special. I am Sacred and Whole. I am pure Divine Energy, Presence and Possibility. I let myself be enriched and enriching! I am delight full!

After writing the statements above, I thought about it while going to sleep that night. I thought about breathing both in and out. To breathe in is Enriching. To breathe out is Enlightening. Or maybe vice versa depending on how you look at it. Maybe we are always being both Enriching and Enlightening. I thought about the word delightful. It is not heavy. It is both light and full at the same time! Maybe that is our essence: DeLightFull!

I thought about the statement: "I am not special. I am Sacred and Whole." We all are. I was surprised how much that lifted my spirit! My birthday was coming up. While I love genuine celebrations, I notice the difference when something feels like an expectation or obligation. Releasing the need to be made to feel special by anyone else enabled me to be free of disappointment from the external.

I am thankful for those that haven't always shown their love for me in the ways I wanted to be loved because I fell in love with myself as a result. I have even had a spontaneous ceremony with myself to accept my whole self in sacred marriage. I said, "I do!" I renewed my vows recently during my D.A.N.C.E. and included "until death do us part if such a thing happens." Maybe my soul dust will live on in the worm that is eaten by the robin and gets wings to fly or in the roots of the trees and become sweet fruit and rich nuts. Oh, my son will like that idea since he thinks I'm a bit of a 'nutter!' I think of the lyrics, "I will be rocks, I will be water" by Deb Talon.

Realizing that none of us are more special than any other doesn't mean that we don't give more attention to some people. There are relationships in our lives that naturally take more of our time and attention, such as parenting. We can still shower people with love! What the realization affects more to me is how we treat those that would not qualify as 'special' to us if we differentiate. Rather, I can remember that we are all Sacred. I enjoy the song, "Blessed We Are" by Peia. It reminds us that we are sacred. It could be another theme song for this book! Remember your life is sacred.

Accepting that I am Sacred and Whole from the inside, no matter what happens from the outside, feels beautiful. I remember when I chose the word 'Sacred' as my word to focus on several years ago. I chose it because it was a way to rearrange the letters from the word scared, as in afraid, and shift the energy and meaning to Sacred. I've noticed a change in my life since then. It seems the words, the energy, and ideas I choose to focus on each year tend to build on one another and weave together and become part of my essence.

A few years later, I chose the word thrive. I was addressing more fears. I had exposed myself to survivalist ideas and conversations. We started prepping to survive who knows what! I still see value in having a wood stove for coziness and for heat if power goes out in winter. Yet, I prefer not to dwell on all of the possible disasters! I made up a word and decided I'd rather be a Thrivivalist. I've even invited Lady Luck to dance and bless me! I invite the Multiverse, as my son calls it, to multiply healthy seeds that grow to fruition, keep a balance, and enable us to thrive in harmony. I trust my ability to give and receive in healthy ways. I breathe in and I breathe out.

Choosing to focus on Sacred rather than Special reminds me I also use the word "we" in affirmations. When military aircraft fly over, I pray, "May we act with wisdom and kindness." I acknowledge my choices relate to all of creation. I use the word kindness purposely to mean 'being of similar origin or species' and 'being considerate.' We're all part of a circle of life here on Earth. I like how "may we" sounds like "mais oui" in French. I translate it 'Oh Yeah' from the French word oui meaning yes. I say YES to wisdom and kindness.

We are Enough and We are Expansive! We are not Special. We are all Sacred and Whole. We are Enriching. We are DelightFull!

I hope and pray that as you continue dancing with life, you are able to see, feel, and accept that you are Enough and you are Expansive in each magic moment of Every day! I hope you can appreciate your own Essence and Muchness. I hope you truly and deeply live and love your life and self! As Lee Ann Womack sings, "I hope you never lose your sense of wonder" and I hope you Enjoy the Dance!

Thank you so very much for sharing this D.A.N.C.E. with me.

AFTERWORD

While working on this book, the Winter Olympics were happening in Pyeongchang, South Korea. I enjoyed watching with my family. My morning D.A.N.C.E. started to look more like figure skating for a while. I heard about 'Going for the Gold.' I think choosing to Dance with Delight is my way of Going for the Gold in Life.

Gold makes me think of the Golden Rule about treating others the way we would like to be treated. I would add to consider how the others like to be treated and to treat ourselves the way we like to be treated, too! Gold also makes me think of *The Golden Compass* book by Philip Pullman. In the book, a golden compass is an instrument that points to truths. I also think about fool's gold. The land, rivers, and driveway where I live all sparkle with it. Gold makes me think of golden honey and treasure chests full of gold. I suppose honey is a treasure collected and created by the bees with Mother Nature.

Treasure was my word cheerleader for 2017. I thought about the verb form of 'to treasure' as in to cherish or value something and also the noun form of 'treasure' that we have or find. I focused on seeing, finding, and appreciating the many amazing treasures both within and around me. I thought about treasuring our lives, loves, and joys. While I was proofreading and editing this book, I kept adding to it. It felt like I was sprinkling more bits of treasure within it, like mica I collect on walks and often forget about in my pockets and purses. It comes out like magical gold dust or fairy dust when I least expect it, such as when paying for dinner or groceries. I wish it could actually pay the bills!

I think Delight is a treasure within us, like a Sacred Fool's Gold. I think Delight can also be a kind of Golden Compass that guides us toward our own inner Truths. Delight is like Golden Honey, which is sweet, nourishing, and medicinal. I think Delight is deeper than a temporary treasure, look, or feeling of happiness on the surface. I think Delight may be the Divine Life flowing through us.

So, I think Dancing with Delight is enlivening. It can be a way to lean in, respect, and honor life. I'm old enough to feel how fast life goes. I have seen enough death to decide that I want to live while I can. I've wondered *What Dreams May Come*. Thankfully, I no longer believe nor fear any kind of eternal damnation. What if that story had never been told? I have read interviews about between lives in *Journey of Souls* by Michael Newton. I've read ideas about having many lives like taking many different dives into a pool of time from the thought provoking and lyrical book, *Crescendo*, by Amy Weiss. I have seen enough death to wonder if it's some kind of mysterious transformation from one form of life to another like a water beetle to a dragonfly or if we rest in peaceful nothingness or recompose in nature. These ideas help me accept and Dance with the mystery.

I remember a wall hanging that I inherited. It belonged to my aunt Denise. I think she made it. She was only 18 when she died a few years before I was born. The wall hanging was pinned to the back of my bedroom door in my childhood home. It had an image of Snoopy, the cartoon dog, joyfully dancing. It said, "Let there be dancing in honor of his name." It noted a biblical Psalm. I think it was referencing Psalm 149:3. It's interesting to me that I saw those words every day during most of my childhood like an affirmation. Years later, I'm writing a book with a very similar idea substituting the word "Creation" or "Love" or "Delight" for "his name."

Let there be dancing in honor of Delight! I wrote the opening poem, *Let There Be Dancing*, after writing most of this book. The poem was partly inspired by the memory of the words from the psalm and my aunt. Let us appreciate, affirm, notice, celebrate, and embrace our mysterious and miraculous magic, beauty, blessings, loves, joys, and lives. Let's ask and invite Delight to Dance with us!

I prefer the idea of offering invitations rather than demanding or issuing challenges! I notice the energy and feeling of various words and ideas. I like the more cooperative and encouraging energy I feel with invitations rather than a competitive feeling and pressure from challenges. Thank you for accepting the invitation to dance with me! May we accept invitations that make our hearts want to sing and dance. May we trust joy and thrive true together in harmony!

Feel free to share the D.A.N.C.E. ritual and invite friends or family to dance along with us. The More, The Merrier! That phrase makes me envision a bunch of merry dancers falling in love with life and drunk on Delight. It makes me think of poetry by Hafiz. You can pass this book on or get another to give when inviting someone to dance. Please credit the source when sharing ideas and respect the copyrights. Writing is part of my liveliness, which is how I prefer to think of business. I am focusing on being lively rather than busy. Still, I have bills to pay. My life's work is to honor, create, explore, celebrate and share sacred beauty and presents in a wild, wonderful world and each of us and encourage others to do the same!

As I finished preparing to publish this book, my father-in-law was back in a hospital. Our neighbor's home was broken into a second time. There was a tragic school shooting where we used to live that impacted friends and co-workers. My dad had a hard fall down the stairs. My husband was stressed about a software product launch that is his responsibility. My cousin's son is trying to recover after having a brain tumor removed that caused neurological damage. There's other violence and despair in the wider world. Life keeps happening. We all have our share of stress. During my morning dance, I said that I refuse to let it steal my peace, joy, and love. I spun around casting a shining circle of loving kindness around me, over this land, and outwards. I pray and affirm, "Let love live here. Let beauty, kindness, grace, respect, and delight be here. So be it."

I think about a quote by Henry David Thoreau that I read in Alice Hoffman's book *The Rules of Magic*: "There is no remedy for love, but to love more." I'm adding, "There is no remedy for life, but to live now" and Dance with Delight when we can! In spite of stress, trespassing, losses, health concerns, disturbing dreams, and heart aches, I lean even more in to joy, love, and life. I lean into what I can trust when it feels hard to trust life. I stand on Mother Earth and I choose to trust my breath in this moment. I gratefully accept a dandelion leaf to eat. I trust a Source that keeps flowing. I let life love me. I start singing my version of "Lovefool" by The Cardigans to life: "Love me, love me. I'll let you love me. Bless me, bless me."

I remember hearing Marianne Williamson say something about wearing rose colored glasses. She said if someone accused her of doing so, she took it as a compliment because it's not always easy in this world. Yes, I have a few pairs of rose colored glasses of my own! I'm reminded of wisdom from a story book I read recently. I think it was *The Witch's Boy* by Kelly Barnhill. One of the characters said something like, "There is no faith without doubt." So, in spite of all my doubts, I still put my faith in love, life and sweet dreams.

I think of lyrics from the song "Gajumaru" by Yaima:

> *"With a brilliant optimism and appropriate ambition*
> *to be open from the center, redirected to the moment*
> *this is it love."*

I don't know if "this is it" as in all there is. Yet, with the many ideas out there about what else might be or happen, it remains a mystery to me. So, I'm going "all in," as they say in poker, with the hand I've been dealt this time around. I'll even bluff to myself to make the most of it if needed. I'm opening and accepting and celebrating the presents of my presence!

Let's Go for the Gold in Life and Dance with Delight!

Echoes of a Fool Moon

~ Julia Ostara

Step In
To the flowing River of Life
Let it wash the Fear Away

Let the Tears Waterfall and Rejoin the Rain
Let the Wind set your hair Wild Again

Breathe In the Scent of the Spring Sap
Ahhh…. Feel the Rhythm in your Blood

Place your Dancing Feet upon the mossy Ground
And let your Head Be in the Clouds
See them Painting the blushing Sky

Bless the Space Between
Where we get to Play in Paradise
Let Heaven be this Place on Earth

Pause
To Appreciate
The Presents of Pleasure

Add your Sweet Soul Song
In harmony with Mother Muse

Be the Sacred Fool
And the Wise Woman
That Celebrate with Gladness

Let Delight Shine Through
The Diamonds of your Pure Essence
To cast Rainbows all Around
As you Return to Love

Rise from the Rich Darkness
To Be You to Full and Bright
Set God and your Wholy Spirit Free

Unbound
Uncaged
Unlimited
Unconditional
Untamed

Untie the Knots
Unlock the Doors

Shed the Old
To Open your Wings
And be Born Again
Like a new Dragonfly

Grow Full and Free and Fabulous
Explore the Wilderness and Wonder
Lift your Self Higher

Feel the Stars Shining in You
See the Sacred gazing back in Your Reflection
Like the Moon in your Eyes
That's Amore

Set Love Free
Leave no one Out
Do a strip Dance
And find the Beloved
Underneath it All

Be the Gold you've been Going for
Hear the Divine Drum in your Heart
Taste the Sweetness on Your own Lips

Let the Seasons be the Clock you Watch
Let Joy be your Compass
Grin and Bare It
Your Laughter is Music
And Medicine and Magic

I'll be your Lovefool

Love Me,
Love Me.
I'll let you Love Me

Bless Me,
Bless Me.
I feel Yah Bless Me

With the Remembrance of Wholiness
And my place Amidst the Tides

I'll Embrace the Hour
And Let it Go
As it Turns my Hands
To Sand to Glass
To a Window in Time

I belong to the Magic of the Moment

I am Divine Delight

~

RESOURCES & REFERENCES

You can find more resources, videos, music playlists, and special offers for readers online at ThriveTrue.com/BookResources

Keep in Touch: www.ThriveTrue.com/MagicMail

The song "Gajumaru" was gladly used as a sort of theme song for the video about this book with permission from Yaima. You can purchase the music if it also touches you at: www.YaimaMusic.com

Book References:
Preface:
Sacred Rebels Oracle Card Deck and Guide Book by Alana Fairchild
Day 2:
Sing You Home by Jodi Picoult
From Anxiety to Love by Corinne Zupko
Big Magic by Elizabeth Gilbert
Alice in Wonderland by Lewis Carroll
To Bless the Space Between Us: A Book of Blessings by John O'Donohue
Day 3:
The Artist's Way by Julia Cameron
Poem Crazy by Susan Wooldridge
Writing Down the Bones by Natalie Goldberg
Journalution by Sandy Grason
Writing Down Your Soul by Janet Conner
Day 5:
Mirror Work by Louise Hay
Wise Women by Joyce Tenneson
Day 7:
Rise Sister Rise by Rebecca Campbell

Blessed are the Weird by Jacob Nordby
Day 9:
Footprints in the Sand claimed by Mary Stevenson, Carolyn Carty or Margaret Fishback Powers
Puddle Pail by Elisa Kleven
Day 12:
A Wrinkle in Time by Madeleine L'Engle
Day 14:
Harry Potter series by J.K. Rowling
Day 15:
Desiderata by Max Ehrmann
Day 16:
Star Wars by George Lucas
Day 18:
The Hobbit by J.R.R. Tolkien
Speaking Peace by Marshall Rosenberg, Ph.D.
Day 19:
Devotions by Mary Oliver
I Heard God Laughing Renderings of Hafiz by Daniel Ladinsky
Where the Sidewalk Ends by Shel Silverstein
Women Who Run With the Wolves by Clarissa Pinkola Estés, Ph.D.
Power of Vulnerability by Brené Brown, Ph.D.
The Birchbark House by Louise Erdrich
Day 20:
Everyday Angels by Mark Kimball Moulton
Invisible Acts of Power by Caroline Myss
Day 21:
Kindness compiled by Sarah Conover
The Tapping Solution by Nick Ortner
Day 23:
Experiments in Truth by Ram Dass
The Gift of Nothing by Patrick McDonnell
Survivor Man television show with Les Stroud
Day 24:
The Power of Myth book by Joseph Campbell
Mythbusters television show
Change Me Prayers by Tosha Silver

Day 25:

Instead of Education by John Holt

The Four Agreements by Don Miguel Ruiz

Dumbing Us Down by John Taylor Gatto

Earthing by Clinton Ober, Stephen T Sinatra M.D., Martin Zucker

Day 28:

New Moon Calendar Journal by April Miller McMurtry

Life Loves You by Robert Holden and Louise Hay

The Biology of Belief by Bruce H. Lipton, Ph.D.

The Power of Intention by Dr. Wayne W. Dyer

The Power of Imagination by Neville Goddard

Day 30:

Avalon Within by Jhenah Telyndru

Afterword:

The Golden Compass by Philip Pullman

Journey of Souls by Michael Newton

Crescendo by Amy Weiss

I Heard God Laughing Renderings of Hafiz by Daniel Ladinsky

The Rules of Magic by Alice Hoffman

A Return to Love Workshop by Marianne Williamson

The Witch's Boy by Kelly Barnhill

Song References (playlist at ThriveTrue.com/BookResources):

Introduction & How to use this book:

"Don't Know Much" performed by Aaron Neville & Linda Ronstadt

"Livin' on the Edge" performed by Aerosmith

"Total Eclipse of the Heart" performed by Bonnie Tyler

"Bust a Move" performed by Young MC

"Dance to the Music" performed by Sly & The Family Stone

Day 1:

"Get Down Tonight" performed by K.C. & The Sunshine Band

"Dancing with Myself" performed by Billy Idol

"With Arms Wide Open" performed by Creed

Day 2:

"Our House" performed by Crosby, Stills, & Nash

"Oh, Yeah" performed by Yello

"Three Little Birds" performed by Bob Marley

"Beautiful Day" performed by U2

"Last Dance" performed by Donna Summer

"Bad Moon Rising" performed by Creedence Clearwater Revival

"Satisfaction" performed by The Rolling Stones

"This Little Light" performed by Emily Riddle

"Glorious" performed by MaMuse

"Feeling Good" performed by Nina Simone

"What a Wonderful World" performed by Israel Kamakawiwo'ole

Day 3:

"Rhyme & Reason" performed by Dave Matthews Band

"Things That Make You Go Hmmm" by C+C Music Factory

Day 4:

"Spread Joy Over This Land" performed by Patti Casey

"Joy to the World" performed by Three Dog Night

"Right Here, Right Now" performed by Jesus Jones

Day 5:

"Good Morning Beautiful" performed by Steve Holy

Day 6:

"Dream On" performed by Aerosmith

"Imagine" performed by John Lennon

"Your Wildest Dreams" performed by The Moody Blues

Day 7:

"Zip-a-Dee-Doo-Dah" performed by James Baskett

"Let It Go" performed by Michael Franti

"Lucky Star" performed by Madonna

"It's Time for Me to Fly" performed by REO Speedwagon

"Howl at the Moon" performed by The Script

"I'm Running with the Wolves Tonight" performed by Aurora

"True Colors" performed by Cyndi Lauper

Day 8:

"You're In My Heart" by Rod Stewart

"All of Me" performed by John Legend

"Footloose" performed by Kenny Loggins

Day 11:

"How Do You Talk to an Angel?" performed by Jamie Walters

Day 12:

"My Wish" performed by Rascal Flatts

"Summertime" performed by Will Smith

"Fortunate Son" performed by Creedence Clearwater Revival

"Signs" performed by Tesla

Day 13:

"Natural Woman" performed by Carole King

"Almost Paradise" performed by Mike Reno and Ann Wilson

"Paradise" performed by Coldplay

"One Sweet World" performed by Dave Matthews Band

"Heal This Land" by Tina Malia

Day 14:

"Unanswered Prayers" performed by Garth Brooks

Day 15:

"Happy" performed by Pharrell Williams

"Addam's Family Theme Song" written by Vic Mizzy

"Beauty In The World" performed by Macy Gray

"Good Vibrations" performed by The Beach Boys

"Sad Songs" performed by Elton John

"Express Yourself" performed by Madonna

Day 16:

"Dance In The Graveyards" performed by Delta Rae

"Into The Mystic" performed by Van Morrison

"Live and Let Die" performed by Guns N' Roses

"The Sounds of Silence" performed by Simon & Garfunkel

"Superstition" performed by Stevie Wonder

"Dancing in the Dark" performed by Bruce Springsteen

Day 18:

"Bring Me Sunshine" performed by Willie Nelson

"Wildflowers" performed by Tom Petty

"These are the Days" by 10,000 Maniacs

Day 19:

"Friend Like Me" performed by Robin Williams

"Life's a Dance" performed by John Michael Montgomery

"Counting Blue Cars" performed by Dishwalla

"Society" performed by Eddie Vedder

Day 20:

"Turning Wake" by Ayla Nereo

"Everyday People" performed by Arrested Development

"Better Together" as Jack Johnson
"We Are The World" produced by Quincy Jones
"Lean On Me" performed by Club Nouveau
"You Sexy Think" performed by Hot Chocolate
Day 21:
"I Believe I Can Fly" performed by R. Kelly
"Have a Little Faith in Me" performed by Joe Cocker
"Rhythm of My Heart" performed by Rod Stewart
Day 22:
"Respect" performed by Aretha Franklin
"Just the Way You Are" performed by Billy Joel
"Every Little Thing She Does Is Magic" performed by The Police
"Masterpiece" performed by Atlantic Starr
"Shower the People" performed by James Taylor
Day 23:
"Show Yourself" performed by Ayla Nereo
"Me and Bobby McGee" performed by Janis Joplin
"Wind Of Change" performed by Scorpions
"Hakuna Matata" performed by Nathan Lane and others
"Uncaged" performed by Zac Brown Band
"Wild Thing" performed by The Troggs
"Wild Again" performed by Jefferson Starship
Day 24:
"Ebony and Ivory" performed by Stevie Wonder and Paul McCartney
"What the World Needs Now is Love" sung by Jackie DeShannon
"Sacred Breath" performed by MaMuse
"Synchronicity" performed by Rising Appalachia
"Shine On" performed by James Blunt
"Free Your Mind" performed by En Vogue
"Man In the Mirror" performed by Michael Jackson
"Shine" performed by Collective Soul
"I Got You" performed by James Brown
"Livin' la vida loca" performed by Ricky Martin.
"Smooth" performed by Santana
Day 25:
"I'm So Excited" performed by The Pointer Sisters
"Book of Love" performed by The Monotones

"A Pirate Looks at Forty" (Mother Ocean) by Jimmy Buffett
"Peaceful Easy Feeling" performed by The Eagles
Day 26:
"Walk of Life" performed by Dire Straits
"Beautiful" by Carole King
Day 27:
"Into The Groove" performed by Madonna
"Go Your Own Way" performed by Fleetwood Mac
"Changes in Latitudes, Changes in Attitudes" by Jimmy Buffett
"I'm Alive" performed by Kenny Chesney with Dave Matthews
"Stayin' Alive" performed by The Bee Gees
"Happy" performed by Pharrell Williams
"So Alive" performed by The Goo Goo Dolls
"Wide Open Spaces" performed by the Dixie Chicks
"Dancing On The Ceiling" performed by Lionel Richie
"What A Feeling (Flashdance)" performed by Irene Cara
Day 28:
"Living in the Moment" performed by Jason Mraz
"Let it Be" performed by The Beatles
"DreamWeaver" performed by Gary Wright
Day 29:
"Twirl Me" performed by Wildlight
"Celebration" performed by Kool & The Gang
Day 30:
"Glorious" performed by MaMuse
"Baby Got Back" performed by Sir Mix-a-Lot
"Shatter Me" performed by Lindsey Stirling
"Rocks and Water" performed by Deb Talon
"Blessed We Are" performed by Peia
"I Hope You Dance" performed by Lee Ann Womack
Afterword:
"Lovefool" performed by The Cardigans
"Gajumaru" performed by Yaima
About the Author:
"Crazy Train" performed by Ozzy Osbourne

ACKNOWLEDGEMENTS & APPRECIATION

This is one of those books that seemed to flow forth in months when really it's the result of my entire life journey thus far. Hence, there are so many people I'd love to thank, some that I don't even know their names. I'm grateful for the variety of people and ideas that have crossed my path, including YOU! Thank you for taking time to read this book, letting me share part of my life soundtrack, soul songs and story with you, and for dancing with me. Once this book leaves my heart to make its own way in the world, it's up to you, the reader, to make of it what you will. You get to determine how successful it is with your choice to read it and, if you feel inspired, to share it with others. Thank you from the depths of my heart and Sacred Spirit for giving it a chance.

I'm thankful for the kindred spirits who agreed to be early readers of this book. Thank you for taking time and sharing your support with me. I appreciate your generous spirits and such sweet words!

I'm thankful for the internet and the friends I've made around the world in online art groups and courses! I'm especially grateful to those that have taken my courses and purchased my offerings. Thank you for your support and healthy exchange of energy!

We share so many collective stories, songs, images, and ideas as we communicate, navigate, and integrate all of our experiences and interactions. Though I'm sure I haven't thought of everyone, here are some of the artists, authors, musicians, healers, and kindred spirits whose inspiration I appreciate: Sark, whose books crossed my path and helped rekindle a creative, wild, wonderful, playful spark within me many years ago. Patti Digh, whose book, *Life is a Verb*, found me soon after my mom died when I needed it most. Kelly Rae Roberts, whose book, *Taking Flight*, also found me soon after my mom died. They both inspired me to dive deeper into the creative process, let art help heal me, and pass it on. That ignited a creative fire that has been warming me from the inside out ever since. That led to an amazing few years of in depth creative courses online and locally. I fell in love with my mixed media art class led by Kristin Steiner and Susan Edmonson at the local John Campbell Folk School in Brasstown, NC. Then, the world of online creative courses opened up to me. In addition to creating and offering my own online courses, I've been blessed to learn with these amazing women: Flora Aube, Ree Altavilla, Alena Hennessy, Kelly Rae Roberts, Tracy Verdugo, Tamara LaPorte, Flora Bowley, Mati Rose McDonough, Faith Evans-Sills, Carrie Anne Moss, and more. I'm thankful for Australian artist, Chrissy Foreman Cranitch. I kept drawing the 'ritual' and 'dance' cards from her Intuitive Wisdom oracle card deck last year, before ever imagining this book.

In addition to authors already listed in the references, I'm grateful for many more. I love great novels and am amazed at the way people can tell such wise, touching stories, such as those by Juliet Marillier, Lois Lowry, Michelle Paver, T.A. Barron, and more. The characters within often encourage me. I love sharing stories with my boys so we can talk about life through them. I'm reminded of advice that stuck with me from a great discussion in the *Kingfountain* series of books by Jeff Wheeler. If I remember correctly, an elder describes two types of wolves within us all, similar to the ideas of good and evil or love and hate or courage and fear. A boy asks the man how you know which one is stronger. The man says that it depends on which one you feed. Indeed! I especially want to thank Kelly Barnhill. I read her book, *The Girl who Drank the Moon*, while writing this book. It was a great way to take a break from writing and the title helped to inspire the title for this book. There are so many authors I've enjoyed that I can't list them all here. I am grateful for all of them and inspiration to write my own book. If you enjoy writing and have thought about creating your own book, go for it! You never know what a blessing it may be to someone or what ripple effects it may have.

I remember an interview when the guest mentioned a book by Hal Elrod and an acronym he used for his miracle mornings. I was inspired to make an acronym for my own morning practice after hearing that interview. I usually did a combination of gratitude pages and writing, visualization, meditation, and movement some mornings at that point. I liked the idea of an acronym to keep it easy and have more structure. I considered many different ones before finding one that made my soul smile. I realized the word D.A.N.C.E. could fit everything I usually did, including the dancing movement that I so enjoyed starting my days with at the time. I'm grateful for the ripple effect from someone I had little knowledge of that helped enrich my mornings and lead to this book.

Many ideas shared within *The Book of Joy* by Desmond Tutu and the Dalai Lama and in *Happiness Now* by Robert Holden have helped me shift old habits and ideas to lean in to joy. I also appreciate the thought experiments from Alan Watts and Tim Freke. I appreciate the Bible interpretations in Ed Bacon's book, *8 Habits of Love*, and Matthew Fox's book, *Creativity: Where the Divine and Human Meet*.

I'm thankful for the musicians already mentioned in the references and so many more that fill my head and heart with music, especially my beloved husband. I love the variety of music in the world. I love to sing and dance along! Music has helped carry me through some rough times and lifted my spirit. I'm grateful for permission from Yaima to use the song "Gajumaru" as a sort of theme song for this book and the video about it! You can support Yaima and purchase the music if it inspires you at www.YaimaMusic.com. The playlist for this book can be found on the additional resources page from my website at ThriveTrue.com/BookResources.

I'm grateful for the local art gallery where my art is shown at Blue Ridge Mountains Arts Association. I'm thankful for every single sweet shop near and far that offers my art, books, and inspiration cards. If you'd like to feature my offerings, please contact me from my website at ThriveTrue.com. I'm delighted to be able to do this.

I'm grateful to Judy Dempsey, the founder of the Summit-Questa Montessori School. She first gave me a chance to try my dream of being a teacher. I loved the experience and the fresh approach to education and community. I'm grateful for the Mary Kay women, Connie, Lisa, Lori, and more that mentored me. You all helped me to see and explore other possibilities and boost my confidence!

I'm grateful for the Magic Mirrors in my life, the friends that have reflected my potential and inner beauty to me when I haven't been able to see it myself. I am grateful for the support from online art friends and kindred spirits, especially those that have collaborated with me to offer courses, e-zines, and interviews. I'm thankful to so many more friends through the years. I especially want to thank my cousin, Jessica, for being one of my biggest fans, the first one to purchase one of my large original paintings for her home, and for singing karaoke with me! I'm thankful to my friend and old dance team buddy, Corinne Zupko, for sharing *A Course in Miracles* and her wise, loving guidance. I'm thankful for my childhood friends, Theta sisters, Gator friends, Blue Ridge Outsiders, Candace, Amy, and all of my "framily," as my dear friend, Jenn, calls friends plus family, for all the love and laughter through the years.

I'm grateful for my brother, Cy, his wife, Keeley, my nieces and nephews, who I love sharing the creative process with! I'm glad to share a love of painting with my Grammie Arlene and my nieces. I also appreciate all the love that my cousin, Monica, has given to my boys, the times she spent babysitting, and our many heart to heart conversations! I'm also grateful to my in-laws for babysitting and love. I'm thankful for the support from the rest of my extended family over the years and lots of merry memories.

I'm thankful for the magicians and inventors of the technology for me to be able to share in videos and printed books and connect with people around the world through the internet! I read a book in *The Great Library* series by Rachel Caine while finishing this. It reminded me how grateful I am for the freedom of speech and ability to share and connect this way. I was also reminded how people from 100 years ago would see the video I made for the book as magic! It felt pretty magical and fun when I was editing it to be able to slow down and reverse the bubbles. The bubble wand even looked like a magic wand. I love the quote by one of my boys' favorite authors, Roald Dahl, about being willing to believe in the magic if you ever wish to find it. I'm glad I can see it and enjoy it!

I am forever grateful for the unconditional love from my mom, Paulette, and the zest for life she shared with me before she died. It continues to shine on, in, around, and through me. I'm grateful for the loving support and encouragement from my dad, Bill. Thank you for being so strong and for loving all of us for Mom, too! I'm thankful for my dad's partner, Jane, who has blessed us twice over with motherly and grandmotherly love.

Most of all, thanks to my husband, Nathan, and my boys, Evan and Drew. You have taught me so much about life and love! You are my greatest gifts and joy. Evan and Drew, I love your hugs, smiles, laughs, jokes, free spirits, curiosity, courage, observations, cat care and expertise, expressions, funny pronunciations, Minecraft ideas, hope, creativity, and stories. Thank you for sharing the world through your eyes with me. Nathan, I'm so grateful to have you as my Anam Cara, my true soul friend. I love singing on Rockband with you! I love all of our intimate conversations. Many of them have influenced this book. I love your touch, your warmth, and your presence. Thank you for putting up with my clutter, creativity, and wild wishes! Thank you for the support to be able to do this! Thank you for your love, your music, and sharing this life journey with me. Thank you for giving me room to grow, explore, and dance. I hope I can return the favor. You guys make my heart sing!

ABOUT THE AUTHOR

I'm an optimystic mountain momma. I live near Blue Ridge, GA amidst the wildflowers with twin boys, a guitar man, a feisty orange tabby cat, a chorus of songbirds, and many woodland creatures.

I am a painter of prayers
Weaver of words
Presenter of presence
Explorer of wild wonder
Lover of life
Mistress of magic
Messenger of mystery
Priestess of possibility

Fluid
Yet strong as stone
And soft as a purr

Raised by fields and woods
Married to my soul

Living with a music man
And growing boys
The fruit of our union
Picked from my womb
Thriving in spite of the odds

~ Excerpt from the poem, "Bits & Pieces of Life, Lace, and Love"

I hope I shared enough of my story in this book for readers to see that I've known grief, violation, and fear yet still choose to dance with delight. I don't share for judgment, attention, or pity. I didn't want to write a 'poor me' book. I feel this book is about power, peace, presence, pure joy and possibility. It isn't about comparing scars. We all have them. I'm not downplaying mine anymore, but I'm not dwelling in the details either. Hence, I shared briefly about some scars that have healed enough to share without spending too much space, time, or energy on details of those events. There are things I didn't share with respect for privacy and my own healing process. I paint and write of the deepest wounds in poetry, which eases the burden for witness and me. I may share more in time.

I never intended to be a healer, but I needed healing for my mind, body, heart and soul. I share my journey because I can, because I have the ability, luxury, and heart to do so, because I'm grateful for beauty, blessings, love and laughter in my life, and because I'm still here. We never know who might be suffering silently. My classmate committed suicide in high school with no warning signs. So, I'm sharing ways I've found to fall in love with life in spite of pain. I'm a survivor of molestation, substance abuse, a party school and a river of grief. Many rather fortunate people experience depression and addiction that contribute to the state of our planet for better or worse. It's time for everyday people to share if we've found ways to heal, feel worthy of choosing joy, and capable of kindness. Maybe a book can be a nonjudgmental and encouraging friend.

I offer creative courses, gifts, art, writing, and wild wishes from my heart to yours. Creative expression helped heal my broken heart. I share many blessings, painted prayers, healing messages, magic, and medicine I've found through art in my inspiration card decks.

While I have a Master's degree, it's not in Art, Literature, or Health, but "Decision and Information Sciences." Though it was like an MIS degree at other colleges, it sounds like it could've been about life choices and exploration! I took a detour from dreams to follow more practical advice and job demand. I worked as a facilitator and project manager in computer consulting when e-business was first starting. I've always been a small town girl at heart and that was quite a different life! I was born on a hippie farm in West Virginia and moved to an island in the Florida Keys when I was 15. When an employer went bankrupt in 2002, I left the profession. My salary plummeted, yet my heart opened when I worked at a Montessori school until I had my kids. Instead of a fine art degree program, I've been blessed to do an on-going self directed art program. I'm grateful for the freedom to choose guides and classes and feel the integration as my art, writing, visions, and creative process evolve! I published the free *Thrive True* e-zine featuring many artists, authors, healers, poets, energy workers, and sweet souls. You can get it free by signing up for emails at www.ThriveTrue.com/MagicMail.

By not taking myself too seriously and shedding cares about what others think, I'm free to explore ideas, do a song and dance show, encourage and entertain. I'm no longer afraid of being a fool! I can sing, "All Aboard" with Ozzy about the crazy train as my train of thought goes off the rails. Still, I'm healing. I wasn't encouraged to follow certain interests growing up because others wanted to protect me from failure, starving, and struggle. As a mom, I get it. As a result, I thought it was too risky or I was too insignificant or untalented to be a successful artist, singer, writer, presenter, etc. Now, I'm taking advantage of the chance I have to try! Vision, voice, wonder, reverence, and love for life may be gifts. I'm trading the fear of failure for faith in my presence, respect for creation, and pure possibility. Willingness to be a Sacred Fool makes me feel like a Wise Woman. We are all artists, life artists.

May we find joy in the art of living and loving, have the courage to beat to our own drums, our heartbeats, to love more not less, to lean in to life, and Dance with Delight. Well Wishes to You!

Julia Ostara
ThriveTrue.com

PREVIEW

Here's a sneak peek into one of my other upcoming books. After finishing this book, I found some words printed out on a piece of paper under my computer. The paper was on the couch where I had been sitting while doing yet another round of editing and proofreading. I'm not sure how it got there! It must have been in my computer bag. I guess it came out when I took my computer out the day before. I started reading the printed words and vaguely recognized them as something I'd written in the past. The words felt like a gift from Sacred Spirit, from my inner magic, messenger, and muse, and from Mother Mystery flowing through me.

Now, I remember when I wrote it. I was sitting with a painting and listening. I was writing about the messages and medicine that came to me through the creative process over several days and weeks spent with the layers of the painting. This is what I mean by the Magic and Medicine Found in Art!

So, that has prompted another book that I've started working on as I finish this one. I see it being a full color book with the paintings and the messages shared together. It felt like this particular message wanted to be included as a preview in this book since it appeared right there with my computer. I'm willing to trust the serendipity and share the message here. The words were written before this book was ever started or imagined. I see how much that painting and the message influenced this book as well! You can see the painting, called Mother Song, from the resources webpage for this book. I hope you enjoy the following preview.

Excerpt from the Forthcoming Book:

Magic and Medicine Found in Art

By Julia Ostara

~~~

The winding road is sometimes actually the easiest and the most beautiful way, such as in the Appalachian Mountains or on Big Sur.

Eat the fruit! Enjoy it, taste it, share it, even when it's messy.

We are all strands of a shimmering, sparkling life song. Learn to harmonize, hold hands, see the depth and gifts and true beauty beneath the surface in selves and each other.

Paint the stars, live in the dream, gathering smiles and tears and honey as the fertile river of gold floods over to quench the thirst of the Earth Mother and all her relations.

Trust the tides of the ocean inside as the plentiful blessings overflow into a purifying waterfall.

Let the fire inside warm your soul and kindle the flames of the divine spark in all who cross your path.

Let the child inside play and wonder and be free to fall and twirl and get back up and laugh and spin again.

Let the Mother Song kiss your lips and guide your steps. Let your heart sing. Let the wild hold you and feed you and wow you. Let the creative juju flow through you staining all that you touch with the fresh blush of joy and exhilaration.

Trust your path and your wellspring and your magic and medicine.

Smell the roses and the apple blossoms. Cast your wishes to the wind upon your breath and watch more bright blooms thrive in your garden. Tend to the Sacred Gathering as a beloved garden flourishing in tune with nature's rhythm beside your fountain.

Smile for me again and again.

Dance with the trees as your bare feet tickle the rich soil.

Let your heartlight be a gift in the dark. Let your laughter and tears and dripping paint and pitcher spill out in ripples across the borders and riverbanks. Trust that you have all you need to honor this life you both give and receive. Let the flood revise the cultural terrain enriching the whole.

Catch the honey and share the sweetness. Cuddle up and rest and replenish. Give yourself room to grow. Bathe in the moon.

Reach to those that reach to you. Dance with the ones that remind you life is a gift, you are a gift and a blessing and a wonder.

Ahhh… let the blessings flow to and through you with ease and grace. Talk to angels and listen to the birds and bees and trees. Let the rainbows embrace you. Close your eyes and open them wide. Feel the sweet stretch when you bend.

Give your sweetest dreams to me to weave and catch the light and each little world in the dewdrops.

Trust life. Love life. Let life love you, too.

See that you are not alone along the road. Re-vision and create the healthy communities you imagine with kindred spirits.

Let the power of kindness spread and the plenty as well. Don't be afraid to be whole, full, and free! Trust yourself. Trust your hopes and dreams and loves and blessings. Lay down the weight of the world as you place your hands upon the Earth.

Turn things upside down sometimes. See the sweet surprises in fresh perspectives.

Be your sweet self... Alive. Remember we are sacred.

Life is now. Pause in the present. Breathe it in deep. Lean in to YOUR life. Let me ripen the fruit for you.

Dance with your shadow until it runs off in the trees to play hide and seek. Find yourself.

You belong to the circle of life. Dive in deep. Let it nourish you.

I love you.

I love me.

I love us.

I love this rich, bountiful, beautiful, wonderful dance and moment.

Mom-ent!

Let me bless your sweet heart.

Let me satisfy your healthy appetite.

Trust us
and healthy harvests and rhythms with audacity and confidence.

~ From the Magic, Messenger, and Mother Muse Within
  (uncensored as it flowed forth)

You can see the painting, called Mother Song, from the resources webpage for this book at: ThriveTrue.com/BookResources

You can sign-up to receive Heart to Heart emails for
Book Release Announcements and Sweet Specials at:
www.ThriveTrue.com/MagicMail

Trust the

Magic

within You

Thrive True